W9-BZT-230

The World's Great Sailing Ships

Originally published as *Les Plus Beaux Voiliers du Monde*
by Éditions Solar, copyright © 1997 SOLAR

English language edition copyright © 1998 by Barnes & Noble, Inc.

This edition published by Barnes & Noble, Inc.,
by arrangement with Copyright S.A.

All rights reserved. No part of this book may be used or reproduced
in any manner whatsoever without the written permission of the Publisher.

1998 Barnes & Noble Books

English translation by John B. Letterman
Text composition and redesign by Gina Webster and Carole Desnoes

ISBN 0-7607-0928-9

Printed and bound in Spain

98 99 00 01 02 M 9 8 7 6 5 4 3 2 1

CAYFOSA

The World's Great Sailing Ships

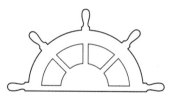

Ollivier Puget

TRANSLATION BY

John B. Letterman

BARNES
&NOBLE
BOOKS
NEW YORK

Contents

Sixteenth-century sailing vessels were rounded in shape, as shown in this 1513 miniature of the Portuguese fleet (ABOVE). The lateen sail remained the most common type.

The galley (ABOVE) with its ram jutting from the prow was the classic warship in the Mediteranean during the Middle Ages. *The France II* (BELOW) is shown under sail in World War I.

From the Galley to Cathedrals of Sail

Since the middle of the 1980s, gatherings of classic tall ships have become more frequent with each passing year, attracting ever-larger crowds who come to stroll on the docks of Saint Tropez, Rouen, Brest, Amsterdam, or Cádiz to admire the world's most beautiful sailing ships and to dream of the lives of their acrobatic sailors.

The perfection of the forms and the riggings of these cathedrals of sail is the result of several centuries of experimentation, adventure, and technical development. While the sailors of antiquity and the High Middle Ages practiced only coastal navigation and daytime sailing, the sailors of the Age of Discovery ventured far into the oceans. Through the seventeenth, eighteenth, and nineteenth centuries, larger and larger vessels were constructed. At the beginning of the twentieth century, record dimensions were achieved in the five-masted French sailing ship, the *France II*, which was put into service in 1913 and measured 128 meters in length.

The steady development of technical capability

Compared to the two millenia that preceded them, technological advances in the seventeenth, eighteenth, and nineteenth centuries were rapid and substantial. Galleys, oar- and sail-propelled warships which were inexpensive to build but of little use outside the Mediterranean, yielded to a range of vessels powered by sail alone.

In the fifteenth century, adversaries at sea sought to dominate each other from high superstructures built as battlements at each end of a ship. These caracks or galleons often carried four masts. The rapid evolution of artillery in the sixteenth and seventeenth centuries brought about changes in the design of these warships and high forward superstructures almost entirely disappeared. The caliber of artillery became more and more heavy and the rate of fire was greatly accelerated. Gun ports were cut into the sides of the ships. In the course of the sixteenth century, effective artillery dueling gradually replaced close-quarter combat and boarding. The techniques of construction and of navigation became more refined. The ram at the prow of the galley developed progressively into a beak or cutwater. Beneath the beak was mounted a carved figurehead, placed there as a vigil to guard a ship against all the dangers that could arise along its route. From the sixteenth to the eighteenth centuries five great powers struggled for mastery of the seas. The Portuguese and the Spanish dominated in the sixteenth century, the Dutch and the English prevailed in the seventeenth. The French at last began to construct their colonial empire at the beginning of the eighteenth century.

The *Euterpe* (ABOVE RIGHT), one of the first great sailing ships constructed of iron plate, sails today under the name *Star of India*. It is the oldest ship still in condition to sail. The stripping down of *Notre Dame de Rumengol* (RIGHT) during its restoration at Brest in 1995–96 revealed its admirable wood framework.

Portuguese and Spanish Expansion

The *Boa Esperança* (ABOVE, TOP) is a scrupulously faithful reconstruction of a Portuguese caravel of the Age of Discovery. It was built in 1990.
A model of Christopher Columbus's *Santa María* (ABOVE, BOTTOM). This is one possible interpretation of his vessel, which was a Catalan nef.

In the fifteenth century the Portuguese sought an ocean route over which to transport the precious spices of the Far East, a route that would circumvent overland trade through the Moslem world which for centuries had interposed a hostile barrier to it.

The Genoese and the Venetians, then the Portuguese, began systematic exploration of the African coast in the fourteenth century. In 1419, Henry the Navigator established a naval academy at Sagres in Portugal. The caravel, a vessel better adapted to the needs of the explorers, rapidly replaced the medieval nef. The caravel was a small ship of forty to sixty tons. It handled well and rose easily into the wind. The Portuguese occupied the Azores in the 1440s and established the fort and trading post of São Jorge da Mina in the Gulf of Guinea in 1481–82. Bartolomeu Dias reached the Cape of Good Hope in 1488. In 1497 Vasco da Gama rounded the Cape and explored the Indian Ocean. From this time onward, the Europeans no longer depended exclusively on the Moslem world for access to the riches of Asia. To avoid the dominant contrary winds along the coast of Africa en route to the East, Portuguese navigators more and more inclined their courses toward the West. This led to Cabral's discovery of Brazil in 1500. At the end of the fifteenth century, the strength of the Portuguese empire rested on its fleet and several important bases. Numerous outposts sprang up along the Brazilian and African coasts and around the shores of the Indian Ocean—Pernambuco, São Tomé, Mozambique, Goa, Calcutta, Malacca, Makasar, Timor, Macao, and others.

During this same time a Genoan, Christopher Columbus, became convinced that the Indies could be reached by a route across the ocean to the West. His contemporaries had underestimated the degree of latitude at forty-five instead of sixty and had also considerably exaggerated the size of Asia. After having been refused by the Portuguese, Columbus succeeded in convincing Isabella I of Castile to finance his risky expedition. Columbus and his three ships finally reached American shores, probably at the site of present-day San Salvador, on October 12, 1492, five centuries after the Vikings had landed at Newfoundland.

From ships of exploration . . .

Historians have acquired a somewhat better knowledge of the ships in use at the end of the Middle Ages. In the Mediterranean, the method of building upon a timber framework had long since replaced the broadside construction first used in antiquity. In the north of Europe, on the other hand, this ancient technique remained in use in the construction of clinker-built boats such as drakkars, whose ribs were set into position after the broadsides were built. In Southern Europe, merchant sailing ships—nefs, caracks, store ships, galleons, for example—were small and round, with a capacity, generally of thirty to forty thousand tons, which rarely exceeded fifty or sixty thousand tons. Their length barely exceeded two-and-a-half to three times their width, as can been observed in the Genoese carack dating from the beginning of the sixteenth century whose excavation was begun in 1982 at Villefranche-sur-Mer in France.

The Armada (RIGHT, ABOVE), **painted by Nicholas Hilliard, is a contemporary depiction of the Invincible Armada of 1588.**
Departure from Lisbon for Brazil, the West Indies, and America by Théodore de Bry (RIGHT). **In this sixteenth-century engraving, one notices the modest size of the galleons destined for long ocean crossings.**

Christopher Columbus (ABOVE).
Ferdinand Magellan (ABOVE RIGHT).
Both portraits are the work of
anonymous sixteenth-century
painters.

This sixteenth-century engraving by
Jan Van der Straeten (ABOVE) represents Christopher Columbus sighting
America. This allegorical vision is a
departure from historical reality.

Thus, we today estimate that the *Santa María* of Christopher Columbus, a Catalan nef, measured approximately twenty-four meters in length by ten meters in width. The ship's sheer was very pronounced, its form big-bellied, the freeboard quite large, the hull strengthened by external upright stanchions spaced from stem to stern, the forward and aft super-structures very high.

Like the Portuguese, the Spanish were quick to replace ships of exploration with merchant ships. In the beginning of the sixteenth century they organized *la volta*. Spanish ships voyaged from Spain by way of the Canaries to the Lesser Antilles to which they trans-ported goods and necessities for the Spanish settlers there. After stopping at Cartagena, Nombre de Dios, and Veracruz, the sailing ships assembled at Santo Domingo (after 1536, at Havana) to return in convoy to Spain, heading for Seville and in later years for the more accessible port of Cádiz. In the early years they especially brought back gold, then silver after the opening of numerous mines,

such as that of Potosí in 1545. The stocks of gold and silver which were available in Europe at the end of the fifteenth century were thereby doubled in the following one hundred and fifty years. The ships of the merchant fleets evolved little, but the size of military vessels increased after the 1560s, in the wake of the revolt of the United Provinces against Spanish rule. The numbers of warships also steadily increased as the competitive struggles of European nations intensified.

. . . to commercial ships

New routes were opened. The Portuguese explorer Ferdinand Magellan found the necessary support in Spain (from an Anvers shipowner) to organize a voyage around the world. He departed from the Spanish port of Sanlúcar, at the mouth of the Guadalquivir River, in August of 1519. After discovering the straits which bear his name, he voyaged to the west and reached the Philippines where he died in an ambush on April 27, 1521. After a voyage of eighty-six thousand kilometers, the circumnavigation of the globe was concluded on September 4, 1522, at Seville, where the sur-vivors delivered 533 stooks of cloves. Of the five ships and 275 men who had set out with Magellan three years before, only one ship, with a crew of eighteen under the command of Juan Sebastián de Elcano, returned to Spain. The supremacy of the Iberians on the high seas took concrete form in 1494 with the signing of the Treaty of Tordesillas, which established the meridian dividing the future colonial possessions of Spain and Portugal.

The entirely gilded prow figure of the Italian training ship *Amerigo Vespucci* (RIGHT) represents the famous explorer. Vespucci explored the Antilles and the coasts of South America.

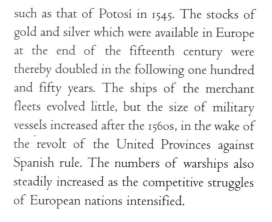

The *Wasa*: From Shipwreck to Recovery

At the beginning of the seventeenth century, Sweden sought to free herself from the hostile grip of her neighbors. A bitter struggle for the domination of the Baltic Sea opposed several countries bordering its shores. Beginning in 1627, Wallenstein, an Austrian admiral in the employ of the Hapsburgs, assembled a fleet of twenty-four warships, purchased or rented from the cities of the Hanseatic League and supported by warships which arrived from Spain. Gustavus II Adolphus, who ruled Sweden from 1611 until 1632, had been at war since 1621 with the king of Poland, Sigismund III Vasa, who had proclaimed his right to the throne of Sweden. The Scandanavian countries therefore had to project a strong naval presence in the Baltic if they wished to continue to navigate freely there.

Faced with these threats, Gustavus II Adolphus resolved to build a squadron of great warships which would be capable of confronting the Hapsburg fleet and its Spanish reinforcements.

At the beginning of the summer of 1628, the efforts of the Swedish naval policy in the Baltic began to bear its fruits. The construction of the sixty-four-gun *Ny Wassamm*, the largest of these ships and the future fleet flagship, was completed. With a displacement of one thousand three hundred tons and a length of sixty-two meters, it could spread one thousand two hundred square meters of sail. On the tenth of August, the *Wasa*—it already carried this name—set out for its first voyage. It was first hauled by cable toward the south along the embankments of Stockholm before it was able to turn and take wind into its sails. A light breeze stirred the surface of the water and four sails were set: the fore and main topsails, the mizzen, and the brigantine. A first small gust of wind caused the ship to heel over; then a second gust, and finally a third one, even stronger, struck the ship. Water entered open portholes and the proud, brightly painted ship sank within minutes. The numerous craft which had accompanied the ship on its first outing hurried to recover the drowning crew. Nevertheless, some fifty sailors perished. An investigation was opened the next day to determine the cause of the catastrophe.

Although there was a strong desire to hold someone responsible, in the end no one was condemned. The cause of the disaster could not be determined precisely. Was the ship too narrow in its beam? Was it insufficiently or poorly ballasted? Were the gunports set too near the waterline? Were orders not promptly enough executed when it was perceived that the set of sail was making the boat heel dangerously?

Over the next fifty-five years, numerous attempts were made to refloat the *Wasa*. The first effort took place on August 13, 1628. In 1663, a Swedish colonel, Hans Albrecht von Treileben, and a diver, Andreas Peckell, formed a team that succeeded in bringing up fifty of the vessel's sixty-four cannon with the aid of

The stern of the *Wasa* as it appears today after restoration. Notice the very rich grouping of decorative elements and statues. The *Wasa* had been designated to be the flagship of the Swedish fleet and its ornamentation mattered as much as its maritime qualities.

an innovative diving bell. The ship was then completely forgotten.

A Swedish engineer, Anders Franzén, rediscovered the existence of the three-decker in 1956. A campaign for its recovery began immediately, and the *Wasa* finally emerged into the open air on April 24, 1961, three hundred and thirty-three years after its sinking. Eight hundred artifacts had already been brought to the surface. Discoveries multiplied after the ship had been raised. The *Wasa* was remarkably well preserved. The low temperature of the water had prevented ship worms from attacking the wood, and mud had conserved the wreck which had settled into a layer of clay thirty-nine meters deep. The pieces that most suffered were objects made of metal and glass.

This was the first time that it had been possible to recover a seventeenth century vessel and to discover, as if by means of a time machine, the lives of the sailors of that era through the objects which they had used.

Twenty years were required to complete the recovery and conservation of the Wasa and to restore and preserve the objects discovered on board. It was an experience of the greatest importance for all subsequent enterprises in marine archaeology and the recovery of ancient ships—both those buried in mud and those simply resting on the floor of the sea.

For its time, the *Wasa* was an immense warship. Two rows of cannon pointed from its hull, and more were positioned on the main deck. Although its sheer was less pronounced than that of the ships of the sixteenth century, its superstructures remained quite high.

The Struggle for Dominion of the Seas

In Northern Europe, the English also participated in the Age of Discovery, thanks to another Italian, Giovanni Caboto, whose name was anglicized as John Cabot, and who was known in France as Jean Cabot. He too was looking for a water route to the Indies, but along a more northerly path. Supported by Henry VII and the merchants of Bristol, Cabot departed from the river Avon in May of 1497 and reached Cape Bonavista in Newfoundland on the twenty-fourth of June. His voyage of discovery was to fix the orientation of British explorers for the centuries to come. Numerous expeditions sought to discover the famous Northwest Passage. The historically researched reconstruction of John Cabot's vessel, the *Mathew*, completed at Bristol in 1995, provides a clear example of the kind of ship into which scores of brave travelers crowded for voyages into the unknown.

A new destination: Newfoundland

Cabot's landfall in North America opened the way to new commerce: the trade in furs and the codfishery. By 1520, approximately one hundred European sailing ships were fishing off Newfoundland. By 1580, this fleet had grown to between four and five hundred ships. At the opening of the seventeenth century their number had grown yet again to around seven hundred ships of fifty to seventy tons with crews of thirty to thirty-five men. English, French, Dutch, Basque, and Portuguese fishermen sailed there each year to exploit the rich fishing banks. This new commerce, although still little known, nevertheless rapidly attracted more men than were required by the Spanish fleets engaged in transporting precious metals from the New World to Seville. After 1540, a triangular commerce developed in Europe. Northern European fishermen, especially those from Brittany, sailed into the Mediterranean to exchange the harvest of the Newfoundland fisheries for alum and other merchandise destined for markets in Northern Europe. Nevertheless, it was Spain that held dominion over the seas in the sixteenth century. Due to its scant population, the Portuguese empire had already began to crumble. Moreover, Portugal itself came under Spanish domination in 1580. The Venetians had lost much of their influence in the Mediterranean. The power of the Turks faded after their defeat in 1751 at the great naval battle of Lepanto, the last in which galleys were used. But other countries to the north challenged the naval supremacy of Spain.

Drake's circumnavigation of the world

Britain enjoyed the services of talented sailors such as Sir Francis Drake in the sixteenth century. In 1585, after attacking the Spanish in the Caribbean, Drake completed a difficult voyage around Cape Horn and entered the Pacific Ocean, which until his arrival had been the exclusive domain of the Spanish. His ship was the one-hundred-ton *Golden Hind*, which had formerly been called the *Pelican*. Drake sailed up the coast of Chile and captured a Spanish ship loaded with gold. He thought to seek a passage to the northeast, around America, by which to return to England, but finally decided to return by a westward route

Francis Drake, by Isaac Olivier (ABOVE).
The compass of Frances Drake (BELOW).

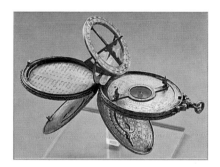

Amerigo Vespucci, by Giulio Romano, painted in the sixteenth century (ABOVE).

The *Mathew* (LEFT). This replica of the ship which John Cabot sailed to Newfoundland in 1497 was constructed in 1995. It sailed to America in 1997, retracing the explorer's original route.

This painting (ABOVE) shows John and Sebastian Cabot preparing to embark at Bristol for the Indies. In fact, it is unlikely that Sebastian Cabot accompanied his father on this voyage.
The English navigator and explorer Sir Walter Raleigh (BELOW).

and crossed the Pacific and the Indian Oceans. After three years at sea, he disembarked at Plymouth, England, in November of 1580 with a cargo of gold and of cloves which he had purchased at Ternate, one of the Moluccas Islands. He had completed the first circumnavigation of the globe by an Englishman. Throughout the sixteenth century, at the same time it was expanding its commercial fleet, England developed powerful naval forces. Great caracks, such as the *Mary Rose* which entered service in 1509 and was refitted in 1536, the *Ark Royal* which was built by Sir Walter Raleigh, or the *Henri Grâce à Dieu* (also known as the *Great Harry*) which was launched with a crew of eight hundred men at Woolwich in 1514 in the presence of Henry VIII, were immense sailing ships of great prestige. The *Mary Rose* sank in the Solent, a strait in the English Channel, in 1545, while coming to the aid of the *Henri Grâce à Dieu*, which French

galleys were attacking. The *Mary Rose*, which was thirty-two meters in length, had a displacement of seven hundred tons, raised four masts, and carried seven hundred sailors and soldiers, is representative of the ships of this period. Its sinking was probably due to a flaw in its design, the portholes having been set too close to the waterline. If the portholes were open when the ship heeled, water could have poured into its hull and sunk it. This hypothesis has been tentatively confirmed by naval archaeologists who have studied the wreck, which has been raised and put on display in the maritime museum at Portsmouth. The *Henri Grâce à Dieu* was certainly the largest ship of its century, with an exceptional length of almost sixty meters. Due to their tall, topheavy riggings, and because they were built to rise high out of the water, these ships were not very seaworthy.

The *Marie la Cordelière*, a carack of François I

of France, confronted the British ship the *Regent* at Camaret Bay at the tip of Brittany in 1512. While maneuvering, the two great ships became entangled with each other and caught fire. These prestigious ships, giants for their time, attest that the nation states of Europe recognized the need to develop powerful naval forces. Nevertheless, these navies were often insufficient and had to rely on the support of private commercial fleets, as was England's case when it confronted Spain's Invincible Armada in 1588.

The end of the Invincible Armada

In 1588, Philip II, at the papacy's urging, constructed the vast fleet known the Invincible Armada and launched it against England under the pretext of reestablishing the Catholic faith there. The incessant attacks of Sir Francis Drake, which had included an attack on Cádiz in 1587 and the destruction of Spanish vessels anchored there, together with the activities of Raleigh and Hawkins, had infuriated the Spanish monarch and fueled the bitter enmity which he felt for Elizabeth I of England. In fact, naval initiative remained with civilians who, like Drake, were highly experienced merchant sailors. Thanks to its merchant marine, England was able to marshal sufficient force to confront the Invincible Armada's sixty-five galleons and other large ships, and its sixty-five smaller vessels. The failure of the Spanish attack definitively confirmed the superiority of naval artillery which had been much improved throughout the sixteenth century. Despite

The *HMS Rose* (RIGHT) is a reconstruction of an eighteenth-century warship. The hull still has a rounded form, but compared to the *Wasa*, its sheer is much less pronounced, the poop deck is lower, and the ornamentation is much more modest.

Human Cargoes

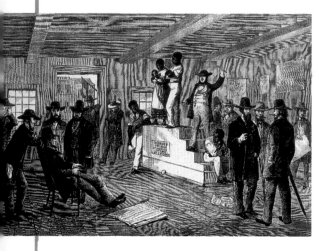

A slave auction at Charleston (ABOVE), from the journal *Universe Illustrated*, circa 1860–61.

The legend of this 1835 engraving, *The Slave Trade* (ABOVE) reads: "What a foul deed—one bargains over what belongs to no one, the other sells what only belongs to Nature." This lithograph of Prétextat Ousel, *Transport of the Negroes to the Colonies* (RIGHT), dates from the nineteenth century.

The slave trade was a complex commerce which exposed a large population to the cruel tragedy of bondage. The commerce in slaves reached its zenith in the eighteenth century. The Portuguese, who required a plentiful and renewable labor force to work their plantations in Brazil, traded tobacco for slaves in Africa. Other nations practiced a triangular commerce. The Spanish imported black slaves to America from 1500 onward. Through contracts called *asientos de negros*, they engaged slave traders to ship black slaves to the Spanish colonies. From the sixteenth to the nineteenth centuries enormous profits accrued to ship owners who gave themselves over to this tragic commerce. The slave trade became a prize for which the great ports of Europe bitterly competed. The French port of Saint-Malo engaged in this trade for a time in the seventeenth century, but it was above all the ports of London, Bristol, Amsterdam, Nantes, La Rochelle, Bordeaux, and Lisbon where the greatest fortunes were made in the eighteenth century.

From the sixteenth to the nineteenth centuries more than 9.6 million blacks were shipped to America. Of this number, the Portuguese imported nearly 38 percent, the English 22 percent, and the Spanish and the French 16 percent. At its height during the eighteenth century, historians have calculated that the slave trade drew off 5 percent of Africa's total population. The impact of the commerce in slaves varied widely from region to region. The most terrible activity was concentrated in Senegal and the Congo.

With the exception of the Portuguese slave trade, the commercial system established by the slave traders was triangular. Ships left Europe loaded with textiles, wines, weapons and firearms, and raw metals such as copper and tin. The traders then exchanged these goods at African trading posts for slaves who were shipped to America in appalling conditions. The slaves were poorly fed and packed into extremely limited spaces, as many as six hundred crowded into boats barely thirty meters in length. Death rates during transit reached 15 percent or higher. When a slave ship arrived at its destination, the slave trader's commercial representative fed and washed the slaves and had their bodies covered with oil to make them more presentable for sale. For the last leg of the triangular commerce, the slave ships took on cargoes of sugar, molasses, rum, tobacco, or coffee, which they transported to markets in Europe.

their maneuverability, galleys were defenceless against well-aimed cannon. The Armada, obsolete at the outset, was commanded by the head of one of the great houses of Spain, the duke of Medina Sidonia, who by his own confession was "incompetant in maritime affairs." After several inconclusive skirmishes in the English Channel, the Invincible Armada, already decimated by a storm, was defeated at Gravelines on August 8, 1588. Only a few rare ships managed to return to port in Spain. This disaster marked the beginning of the decline of Spanish naval supremacy. Nevertheless, the empire of Philip II, despite the loss of several possessions—notably in the Antilles to the profit of the English, the French, and the Dutch—was to preserve Spain's commercial preeminence for many years.

The passage to India

At the end of the sixteenth century, Sir Francis Drake disputed the Spanish and Portuguese commercial monopoly in Asia on behalf of Elizabeth I's England. The United Provinces, created from the seven provinces of the Low Countries which in 1594 had won independence from the rule of Philip II's Spain, were also eager to engage in overseas trade. A first expedition of four armed ships, supported by a group of nine Amsterdam merchants, set out for Asia from Texel Island on April 2, 1595, under the direction of Cornelis Van Houtman. Of the two hundred forty-nine sailors only eighty-seven returned to Holland in August of 1597, bringing with them a cargo of pepper. The company formed by the nine merchants made no profit from the voyage, but trade with the East had been opened to the Dutch. By 1598, five companies had formed, assembling twenty-two vessels for trade with the Far East. To avoid competition among the companies, which would have led only to

higher prices, the Parliament of the United Provinces issued a charter which organized the five companies into one. On March 22, 1602, the Verenigde Oost Indische Compagnie (VOC), the Dutch East India Company, was born—rival to Britain's East India Company. Elizabeth I had granted the EIC the right to trade in the East in a charter, signed by her hand and dated December 31, 1600. The first expedition of the Dutch East India Company set out immediately for Malaysia. In 1619 the Dutch built a fort, which they named Batavia, on the island of Java, near the city of Jakarta. Several months later they fought off the British who had beseiged them there, took the neighboring city, and annexed the kingdom.

While the East India Company was an enterprise similar to many other English commercial enterprises of the time, the Dutch East India Company had been granted privileges like those of an independent state. The Company minted coins, established an army, constructed fortifications, and negotiated and signed treaties. It was financially organized with a fixed capital. The first dividends were not to be distributed until ten years after the Company's formation. In contrast, the East

In April 1995, Willem Vos, after ten years of work, christened the *Batavia* (ABOVE), a faithful reconstruction of a seventeenth century ship of the Dutch East India Company. The lion figurehead at the prow, gleaming in gold leaf and vivid paint, has been faithfully reproduced.

Several tools used for navigation in the modern era (ABOVE): a globe, an astrolabe, a cross-staff, a John Davis's backstaff, an hourglass, and a map.

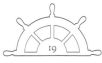

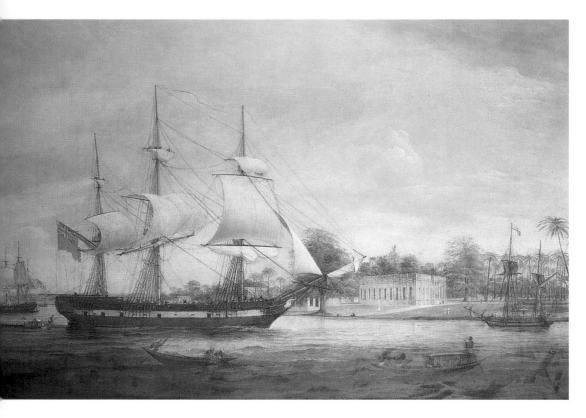

A three-masted ship in the estuary of the Hooghly River near Calcutta, by **Thomas Whitcombe** (ABOVE). **By the nineteenth century, the English had long replaced the Portuguese in India.**

A bitt (or bollard), wood or metal post around which is wound a hawser, on the poop deck of the *Belem* (ABOVE). Setting a studding sail on the *Pride of Baltimore* (ABOVE RIGHT).

India Company divided profits as soon as ships returned from their voyages, which was the common practice at the time.

Like the Portuguese a century earlier, the English and the Dutch established trading posts in India and throughout the East Indies. The East India Company and the Dutch East India Company formally agreed to regard Portugal as their common enemy and Portugal consequently lost most of its settlements in the seventeenth century. By the second half of the century, there remained of Portugal's colonial empire only Goa, Macao, a part of Timor, the present day nations of Mozambique and Angola, and, most importantly, Brazil. By that time, the Dutch fleet had grown to an aggregate of about four hundred thousand tons to become the largest in the world. Between 1612 and 1616, the Danes also attempted to establish trade in

Asia, but their efforts were fruitless. In the middle of the sixteenth century, France also sent ships out to the Indies. Jean Ango, for one, a wealthy shipowner from Dieppe, in 1529 mounted an expedition of two small twenty-meter ships, the *Sacre* and the *Pensée*. Although the expedition reached Sumatra, it returned with only a few tons of pepper and was a failure. At the end of the sixteenth century, a certain Duquesne, an ancestor of Abraham Duquesne, brought back a cargo of precious spices from the Moluccas Islands. But these expeditions remained the incidental work of adventurers. In the seventeenth century, the French had no lasting success in the Far East.

The Dutch and the store ship

During the seventeenth century, the Dutch developed numerous high performance vessels and became the world leader in commercial navigation. A type of craft known as the store ship replaced the trading ships of the late Middle Ages. Its innovative design made it possible to reduce the size of its crew and to carry more freight. It could also be fitted with artillery. Store ships were about forty meters long with low fore and aft superstructures, which reduced the tophamper and made them more seaworthy. This type of vessel was soon imitated throughout Europe. The English, after losing a number of their sailing ships during the first Anglo-Dutch war (1652–1654), copied them with great precision.

La Recouvrance (ABOVE RIGHT), **a reconstruction of a schooner dispatch boat of the nineteenth century.**
The Victory, **a late-eighteenth-century ship of the line** (RIGHT), **on which Admiral Nelson died. Today it is at Portsmouth, England.**
The Royal Flotilla, **by Dominique Serres** (FOLLOWING DOUBLE PAGE).

The Birth of National Fleets

Throughout the sixteenth century, further enormous advances were achieved in the science of navigation and in maritime technologies. Navigation, which before had been empirical, developed into a mathematical, astronometric, and cartographic science. While the Portuguese and the Spanish attempted to reserve for themselves the secrets of quickly evolving maritime technologies and the science of navigation, the popularization of new knowledge, especially among the Elizabethan English, made new scientific discoveries available to a wide audience of autodidacts. In England, this fostered the training of numerous navigators and led to a broad acculturation of the commercial maritime power of the country. On the other hand, the development of national fleets in the seventeenth and eighteenth centuries was slowed by the enormous cost of shipbuilding and the even greater costs of maintaining the ships and their crews. After each campaign a ship's rigging had to be entirely overhauled. The number of sailors required for a fleet ranged from fifty thousand to sixty-five thousand. Only England, with no land borders, could concentrate its military resources on its navy. In France, during the War of the League of Augsburg, when Louis XIV had to confront a coalition uniting Austrian and Prussian land forces on the one hand, and English and Dutch naval forces on the other, his dispersed efforts to meet both challenges led to defeat. The Treaty of Ryswick ended the war in 1697 and obliged Louis XIV to give up almost all the territories that he had conquered since 1685.

England also enjoyed several decisive infrastructural advantages over France. England had a sound fiscal system and a bank through which its government could borrow money, as well as a command system that left ample room for initiative to its admirals. In France, on the other hand, taxes weighed almost exclusively on the peasantry and were difficult to collect. There was no central bank and the currency in circulation was weak. Finally, the French military hierarchy was extremely centralized. Decisions were made by the king and the naval ministry, allowing fleet admirals to exercise little initiative.

The officer of His Majesty

A naval ministry was developed in France during the sixteenth and seventeenth centuries. The first French sailors were private adventurers who knew the ways of the sea. High command, on the contrary, was the prerogative of high-ranking nobles whose training was in land warfare. Beginning in 1627, Richelieu, then Colbert and Seignelay, the son of the latter, pursued policies aimed at creating a highly centralized national navy. Richelieu concentrated powers in his own hands. Specific training was organized for the future officers of the navy, which led to the formation of naval guard companies at Brest, Rochefort, and Toulon. By the end of the seventeenth century, Richelieu and Colbert had replaced self-taught sailors of humble origins with officers drawn from the nobility and trained in state naval schools. The new corps of officers commanded ships constructed in royal shipyards.

From the *Atlas of Colbert* (1679) Plate 10, *Pinnaces of La Rochelle, Views from the Poop Decks* (LEFT).

Portrait of Cardinal de Richelieu, painted by Philippe de Champaigne in 1636 (ABOVE).

Portrait of Colbert, attributed to Claude Lefebvre (ABOVE).

The Rise of European Navies

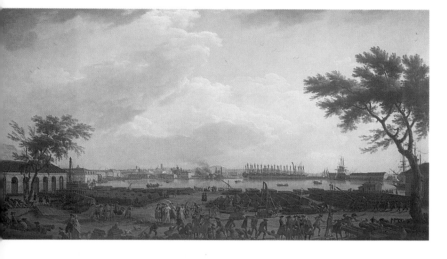

The shipyard at Toulon, painted by Joseph Vernet (ABOVE). In 1753, Louis XV commissioned Vernet to paint views of the principal ports of France.

An eighteenth-century portrait of Peter I (the Great) by Ivan Nikitin (LEFT). Czar Peter I founded the Russian navy.

The fleets of merchant sailing ships in seventeenth-century Europe were not composed of ships well suited for long voyages. Only a few very rare large warships were more than sixty meters long with twenty-five hundred to three thousand tons of displacement. These carried crews of several hundred men. Merchant ships, on the contrary, rarely exceeded one hundred tons. Shipowners sought, above all, to minimize their costs by limiting the size of the crews.

In 1664, Colbert initiated a major survey whose goal was to determine the size and characteristics of the French merchant fleet. The survey estimated a gross tonnage at 150,000 for the French fleet, compared to a tonnage of 200,000 for the British fleet, and a tonnage of 500,000 for the Dutch fleet at the time. The French fleet was composed primarily of ships of very small tonnage. Ships of two hundred fifty to five hundred tons, which were capable of extended voyages, represented only 2 percent of the total. The proportion of large ships to small was certainly greater in Spain, the United Provinces, and in England during this period, but the French would close the gap in the eighteenth century.

Most European sailing vessels in the seventeenth century were small coastal craft. Some were capable of coastal navigation over relatively long distances—as far as the Baltic for the ships of the Western Mediterranean, and throughout the entire Mediterranean for ships based in its eastern waters. Trade with the Baltic flourished. Merchants from the western Mediterranean, especially, voyaged there to take on cargoes of grain. When bad harvests in Europe gave rise to shortages and famine, cereals from the plains of Poland and Russia were in great demand until the next harvest.

The Baltic: wealthy nations . . .

The countries bordering the Baltic Sea also supplied the West with the raw materials needed for the construction of ships. The mainmast of a sixty-four-gun ship of the line rose seventy meters from the keel of the ship to its top. Because no trees of that height existed, masts had to be divided and built in several parts. Lower masts were generally thirty-three meters in length and ninety-two centimeters in diameter. Only the great pines of the Scandinavian north possessed the size, flexibility, and strength required. Scandinavia produced not only this indispensable timber but also the pine pitch, tars, and resins needed to waterproof hulls. Poland and the Baltic countries supplied flax and hemp, Russia and Sweden provided iron and copper. Holland, especially, but also England and the Iberian peninsula, needed great quantities of these raw materials—which they did not have in their own territories—for the development of their navies. The supplies of naval stores depended essentially on the Baltic countries.

The *Norden* (ABOVE), a Baltic coastal vessel, launched in 1870. The square-rigged, three-masted Italian training vessel, the *Amerigo Vespucci* (LEFT), launched in 1930, was built in the style of ships of the mid-nineteenth century.

The *Batavia* at Sail Amsterdam '95 (ABOVE), a reconstruction of a ship of the Dutch East India Company.

Many navies also purchased Swedish cannon, which were reputed to be the best in Europe.

In the sixteenth and seventeenth centuries, ships primarily entered the Baltic to take on cargoes of raw materials. Many of these ships made the first leg of their journeys carrying only ballast. At the end of the seventeenth and in the eighteenth centuries, the number of ships traveling empty to the Baltic diminished as Eastern European countries demanded more and more goods from the West and the colonies. The English exported cloth to the Baltic region, and the countries of Southern Europe exported ever larger quantities of salt, oil, wine, and other products. The Dutch increased their exports of spices and exotic products. Sugar became an increasingly popular commodity in Europe, as well.

. . . but coveted

The Baltic Sea was also the setting of numerous rivalries in the seventeenth and eighteenth centuries. The ambitious policies of Gustavus II Adolphus and his successors sought to control maritime commerce. Sweden conquered Finland, Estonia, Karelia, Livonia, and, most importantly, Pomerania. By 1660, the Baltic had become a Swedish lake. But new powers were emerging. From

the beginning of the reign of Charles XII (1697–1718), Czar Peter I and the kings of Poland and Denmark entered into an alliance to retake from Sweden the territories that it had conquered and occupied.

Russia's opening to the sea

Russia was exclusively a land power at the start of Peter the Great's reign. Its territory touched neither the shores of the Baltic nor the Black Sea. Nevertheless, Russia's domain was vast, stretching from the Caspian Sea to the White Sea and reaching across Siberia to the Pacific. Trade moved across land through a port on the White Sea at Archangel, which was opened in 1584. The port, however, was only served by foreign ships and was accessible only in summer. Peter I, who had been introduced to naval construction at an early age, believed that access to the sea was the source of the wealth of the countries of Western Europe. He decided that Russia needed ports and a fleet of merchant ships. He sought first to reconquer the territories bordering the Baltic and the Black Seas. But the difficulties he had experienced in taking the Turkish fortress of Azov in 1696 convinced him that he also had to acquire a fleet of warships. A ukase adopted by the Duma of Boyars on October 20, 1696, authorized the formation of the Russian navy.

The Czar soon set off on a trip to all the countries of Europe except France. In 1697–98, he visted the United Provinces and England to study naval techniques and marine construction. He recruited Dutch ship carpenters, then reputed to be the best in Europe, naval architects, and navigators and sailors whose task would be to train Russian officers and crews. Nevertheless, for many years afterward, the Russian navy was commanded by officers of foreign nationality. In 1700, Peter I declared war on Sweden, which then dominated the Baltic and which had taken possession of Livonia during the first northern war between Czar Alexis Mikhaylovich and Sweden's King Charles X.

Saint Petersburg and the triumph of the Russian navy

Peter I lost the first battle of the Great Northern War on November 19, 1700. He soon understood that confrontation with Sweden's naval forces would decide the outcome of the war. In 1703, he reached the mouth of the Neva River at the source of the Gulf of Finland. A fortress, christened Peter and Paul, was quickly built there, as was another one, more to the west at Kronschlot, which was renamed Kronstadt in 1723. The city of Saint Petersburg quickly sprang up around the first fortifications. The new city served as the base for the gradual reconquest of territories to the south of the Gulf of Finland. On June 27, 1709, the Russians won a decisive victory against Sweden, which marked the beginning of the decline of Swedish naval power. In 1712, Saint Petersburg became the capital of the Russian empire. A Russian naval victory in 1714 confirmed that the Czar's fleet could stand up to the Swedish navy.

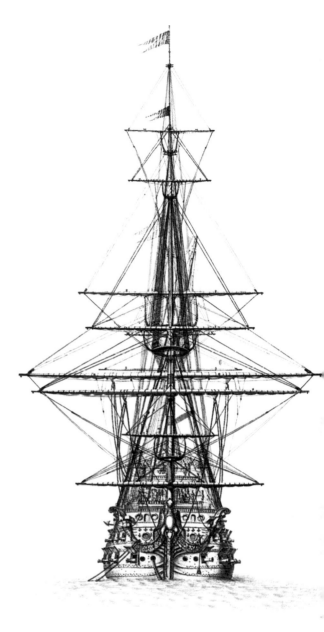

Plate 49, *Prow of a Vessel at Anchor* (ABOVE), from the *Atlas of Colbert* (1679). Note the top mast on the bowsprit and the yardarm of the spritsail, which is a large square sail that is rigged under the bowsprit.

The *Tovarishch* (LEFT), seen from its bowsprit during a tall ship race in the North Sea in 1993.

The three-masted Portuguese training bark, the *Sagres II*, on starboard tack (FOLLOWING DOUBLE PAGE).

The Evolution of Naval Hygiene

Hygiene aboard ships that made prolonged voyages had always been disastrous. On the longest journeys, ships often lost 20 percent or more of their crews. A sailor's life was defined by overcrowded and unsanitary conditions, an unbalanced diet of often rancid food, and a lack of ventilation that incubated epidemics. Observers at the time ascribed the rate of mortality to the "piling up of men," "poor ventilation" and its corollary, "humidity that infected men with rot," and, of course, the impossibility of keeping food provisions fresh. The situation was still worse on warships, where the sailors were even more intensely crowded together. The *Soleil Royal*, the flagship of the fleet of Louis XIV, embarked with crews numbering from nine hundred to one thousand men, although the design of the ship had only provided for a crew of eight hundred sailors. The living spaces reserved for the crew were encumbered with a diverse range of objects: the personal effects of the sailors, artillery pieces, rope, provisions, water, and the many things that could not be stowed elsewhere. The height between decks was limited; men could not stand upright. To make matters worse, it was common to see animals crowded on the decks of ships departing for long voyages. These poor conditions jeopardized the health of the crews, upon whom a nation's safety and wealth relied.

One compensation for the deplorable quality of the food was alcohol: beer, cider, or wine, depending on the country. In the eighteenth and nineteenth centuries, this regimen was supplemented by much stronger spirits, such as rum. The Swedish admiralty allowed each of its sailors a ration of seven liters of beer per day!

In the second half of the seventeenth century, hospitals for sailors were built at the great French naval bases. Medical schools were established at the beginning of the eighteenth century, but the surgeons who emerged from them were powerless against the many epidemics that decimated the crews. Health officials realized that frightful rates of shipboard

Lithograph of a view of a battery in an early-nineteenth-century vessel, by Morel. Notice the sailor in his hammock.

mortality had impaired the military effectiveness of their nations' navies. When crews died like snowflakes melting in the sun because of epidemics, the success of military operations such as blockades was put at risk. In fact, many more sailors died from problems of hygiene and disease than died in battles or in shipwrecks. It is estimated that Britain's royal navy lost seventy-five thousand men to disease between 1756 and 1763. Faced with these grim statistics, surgeons, doctors, and admirals in England and in France realized that it was imperative to take steps to prevent disease.

In 1795, as part of England's disease prevention efforts, the British admiralty required its crews to drink lemon juice to help curb scurvy, a major health hazard. The British also identified another main threat to healthful conditions at sea, when Dr. James Lind pointed

out in 1757 the necessity of keeping water fresh during long voyages. The admiralty's initiative helped the British navy sustain the blockade of France that contributed to the final defeat of Napoleon in 1815. In France, Bigot de Morogues, the father of the French naval academy, suggested that sailors' clothing be heated in stoves to kill the vermin that infested them, such as the lice that transmitted exanthematous typhus, then known as "ship fever." Ship fever killed about ten thousand persons at Brest, in 1757–58.

Efforts were also made to improve ventilation. An Englishman named Hales invented a blower to ventilate the holds of ships. Bigot de Morogues studied the invention and proposed modifications, but the technology required to install the system did not yet exist. One problem, for instance, was the reliance on leather pipes—which rats destroyed—for ventilation conduits. It was not until the nineteenth century that shipboard living conditions were truly improved, thanks to better ventilation, increased living space for sailors, and great strides in medical prevention and treatment.

The Apogee of Sail

At the end of the eighteenth century, in France as in England, the average displacement of merchant ships was around one hundred tons and only rarely attained as much as one thousand tons. During this period, the evolution of the sailing ship was most remarkable among naval vessels, the largest of which displaced three thousand tons. Navies developed at the end of the seventeenth century and throughout the eighteenth century. The recruitment of crews was organized, the hierarchy of command was put into place, shipyards were established, shipbuilding techniques were developed, and the tactics of sea warfare were refined. Artillery had already assumed an importance greater than that of maneuver. The number of gun crews determined the size of the crews. Boarding and hand-to-hand combat were replaced by confrontations between the artillery of two fleets. Warships were divided into five categories, according to the weight of their artillery and the number of their decks. A ship of the line of the first rank carried between seventy and one hundred twenty cannon; of the second rank, between sixty-two and sixty-eight cannon; and so on. The most advanced of French warships, admirably designed by Jean Boudriot, carried seventy-four cannon. But this categorization, which was established in the middle of the seventeenth century, concealed great disparities.

Victory at Trafalgar

The only ship of the line still extant is the three-decked *Victory*, preserved today at Portsmouth, England. This vessel carried 102 artillery pieces. It was launched in 1765 at Chatham and was the flagship of Admiral Nelson at Trafalgar. Nelson died on board on October 21, 1805, during the sea battle in which the Franco-Hispanic fleet was crushed. Two other sailing vessels built at the end of the eighteenth century have been preserved, the frigates *Constellation* and *Constitution*, which were the first warships built by the young American nation after winning its independence. They are today open to the public at Baltimore and Boston, respectively.

The great explorations

The eighteenth century was also a period of important progress in navigation. After 1730, the octant replaced the cross-staff for the calculation of latitude, and was itself replaced by the sextant in 1750. But the calculation of longitude remained a major problem. The first person to perfect a reliable chronometer was an English clockmaker named John Harrison. In 1773 he was awarded the prize of twenty thousand pounds, offered by the Board of Longitude in London, for his famous H4 clock, which could keep time to the second during long voyages. Two French clockmakers, Pierre Le Roy and Ferdinand Berthoud, made important improvements to Harrison's chronometer. By the end of the century, the clocks lost less than one second of time during expeditions which lasted a year. These advances made possible the preparation of precise maps by the numerous expeditions that crisscrossed the globe during the second half of the eighteenth century. But, even at the end of

Contemporary portrait of Louis Antoine de Bougainville (ABOVE).

Posthumous portrait of Captain James Cook (BELOW) painted circa 1800, by Sir Nathaniel Dance Holland.

The Victory at Portsmouth, by Albert
Goodwin (ABOVE). A view of the
naval dockyard; the Victory appears
behind a frigate.

the century, few ships benefitted from this progress. Merchant ships, especially, continued to use older methods of navigation, either because of a distrust of innovation or the lack of means to procure new equipment.

The progress in shipbuilding and navigation technologies, engendered by the development of navies, made it possible to undertake ambitious maritime explorations with greater chances of success than those of the sixteenth century. The motivations behind these voyages of discovery were not exclusively economic. Exploration of the Pacific became systematic with the annual passage of the Manila galleon that crossed the ocean to transport products from the Philippines to America and then to Spain. Whalers, in search of new hunting grounds, also explored uncharted waters. Curiosity, too, motivated explorers and governments, which alone could finance large-scale scientific expeditions. Seafaring explorers led many important expeditions in the latter half of the eighteenth century: Bouganville (1764–69), James Cook (1768–78), La Pérouse (1785–88), to name a few. Most of the planet had been explored by the end of the century, with the important exceptions of Central Asia, Central Africa, and Antarctica, which was first reached by several explorers between 1819 and 1821, and was explored by Dumont d'Urville between 1837 and 1840. The planet thus became a finite world that could be comprehended in its entirety.

Lithograph representing the French navigator Jules Sébastien César Dumont d'Urville's passage of the polar circle (LEFT).

On board the Mariette (RIGHT).
The parrel, a set of sliding rings which secures the sail to the mast when the sail is hoisted. Note the leather bindings.

The *Endeavor*, launched in December 1993 in Fremantle, Australia, is a reconstruction of the ship which Lieutenant James Cook embarked in 1768 for his first voyage of exploration in the South Pacific. The vessel circumnavigated the globe in 1997, and has attended many gatherings of sailing ships—here in Sydney (OPPOSITE). Above, a detail of the mizzen-mast. Note the bright colors and the importance that was still given to decorative elements at the end of the eighteenth century.

The Age of Giants

The mainmast of the *Belem* (ABOVE), launched in 1896. In the course of the nineteenth century the spread of sail was divided in two, resulting in a lower and an upper topsail.

The *Duchesse Anne* (BELOW), which served as a German training ship, was surrendered to France after World War II. It long served as a floating school for the French navy. Now restored, it is in Dunkirk.

At the dawn of the nineteenth century, larger merchant ships were at last being built, and commercial sailing craft of more than one thousand tons became more common. The living space available for each sailor increased and conditions on board slowly improved. After the American War of Independence, commercial activity between Europe and North America developed. Numerous ships were built, thanks to the immense American forests that were within easy reach of naval shipyards. In 1818, the Black Ball line opened the first regular transatlantic service between New York and Liverpool, which ushered in a new era of ocean transport.

New and faster three-masted ships appeared in the United States and Europe. These streamlined boats were slender, rapid schooners, shaped for racing. Their rigging had been divided, and their sail surface had been increased. Naval architects and shipbuilders now labored to design boats for speed. A name derived from an English word, to *clip*, meaning to cut, was applied to these ships, and their hulls did indeed slice through the water as the older round-hulled merchant vessels had never done. The first "clipper" ship was the *Rainbow*, an American square-rigged three-master that John Willis Griffith put into service in 1845. The naval architect's principal concern had been to reconcile speed with his ship's capacity to carry freight. In 1848, the discovery of gold in California attracted one hundred thousand immigrants to the West Coast. Their voyage around Cape Horn was difficult, but for them the crossing by clipper ship was preferable to the slow and dangerous overland route. Soon afterward, in the 1850s, the clipper ships transported other emigrants, this time drawn to Australia by another gold rush. These ships were built in ever-larger sizes. The Boston shipyard of Donald Mac Kay launched some of the most famous of these, ships such as the *Flying Cloud* and the *Great Republic*. These grand vessels, with four masts and lengths of more than one hundred meters, were the largest clipper ships ever built.

Speed above all

The English and the French reacted to this new competition from America. An innovation in the 1850s made it yet again possible to improve the performance of sailing ships: a wood exterior built over a framework of metal. This made it possible to increase a ship's length in proportion to its width and to reduce construction costs. The *Mineiro* was the first ship of this type. It was launched at Bordeaux in 1852 by Lucien Arman. Shipyards at Nantes and Bordeaux proceeded to refine this technique of shipbuilding. The first ship constructed of composite materials in England was the *John Lidgett*, launched at Glasgow by Alexander Stephen & Sons, on August 29, 1862. These clippers broke record after record thoughout the decade. They were put in the service of various passenger lines that carried relatively light freight that required rapid delivery. The famous races known as "tea races" inspired competition among the well-known English clipper ships, the most celebrated of which were the *Thermopylæ* and the *Cutty Sark*, which was launched on

November 12, 1869. When their raison d'être—their speed in transporting tea from Shanghai by way of the Cape of Good Hope—disappeared with the opening of the Suez Canal and the development of steam propulsion, they were assigned to the shipping trade in Australian wool. It was on this route that the *Cutty Sark* broke speed records.

Prestige, yachting, and the regatta

With the industrial revolution appeared another new form of sailing: yachting. Many of the great bankers, industrialists, and royals of the nineteenth century built prestigious sailing yachts for pleasure travel. Among the most famous of these is the schooner *America*, whose crew flouted its English competitors at Cowes, in 1851, and won the Hundred Guinea Cup. This is the origin of the America's Cup. The regatta developed a wider appeal during this period. The desire to build luxurious vessels gave rise to some creative shipbuilding endeavors. For example, in 1921 the Duke of Westminster purchased the hull of a destroyer that the Italian navy had put into dry dock. He transformed it into a four-masted private yacht and christened it the *Flying Cloud*. After changing hands several times—at one point it belonged to Lord Guinness, who also owned the *Belem*—it sails today as a cruise ship in the Antilles. But certainly the wildest dream was achieved by the American financier Edward Francis Hutton, who commissioned the largest yacht ever launched, the *Hussar*. Later, when divorcing, he offered it to his wife, who renamed it the *Sea Cloud*.

The last century also saw the adoption of steam as the principal means of propelling larger ships. These vessels were often constructed with iron hulls. The first sailing ship of this type was launched in England in 1840 and was named *Vulcan*. In 1839, the English naval architect Isambard Kingdom Brunel designed a revolutionary new iron-hull vessel equipped with a steam engine, intended to be a transatlantic passenger ship. Brunel decided to install propellers instead of paddle wheels on his new ship, which he named *Great Britain*. Launched in 1843, the innovative *Great Britain* had a troubled history—running aground, a refitting to run purely on sail power—before it was abandoned in the Falkland Islands. Brought back to England and restored, it is today docked in Bristol, and is open to the public.

In November 1859, France launched a new ship of war, a three-masted bark, the ironclad frigate called the *Gloire*. It was constructed of wood which was covered with armor-plate 120 millimeters thick, and was fitted with a steam engine that could propel the ship at a speed of thirteen knots. The *Gloire*, very advanced for its time, relegated all other warships to the rank of museum pieces. The British responded while

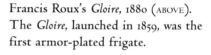

Francis Roux's *Gloire*, 1880 (ABOVE). The *Gloire*, launched in 1859, was the first armor-plated frigate.

The crowned stern of the English clipper *Cutty Sark* (ABOVE). Today restored, it resides in Greenwich and is open to the public. It houses a fine collection of prow figureheads.

This view of the masts of the *Sea Cloud* (ABOVE) shows the metal spars and the steel cables that have made it possible to raise taller masts and, consequently, to spread more sail.

Photograph of Jean-Baptiste Charcot (BELOW).

the *Gloire* was still under construction, conceiving the *Warrior*, whose keel was laid even before the *Gloire* was launched. The naval architect Isaac Watts designed—with the aide of Thomas Lloyd, who had studied Brunel's work and had taken part in the maiden voyage of the *Great Britain*—a sailing ship of an entirely new conception. He built the ship around an armored central parallelepipedic rectangle that housed the gun batteries. The *Warrior*, launched in 1861, was propeller-driven and powered by a 1,250 horsepower steam engine. It measured 118 meters in length and displaced more than 9,200 tons. It is presently on view in Plymouth, England, fitted out as it was originally.

By the close of the century, mechanical propulsion had definitively superseded sail power, and warships appeared without riggings. Commercial sailing craft persisted longer. Construction in metal developed in England after 1853 and then spread throughout Europe. Metal construction technology allowed for faster, more economical ships that could carry more freight. Metal masts soon replaced the former wood spars; and steel cables took the place of hemp for the shrouds and stays. The spread of sail expanded as the number of masts multiplied. The adoption of steam-powered winches made it possible to operate larger sails without a more numerous crew. New records were set in the 1880s.

The America's Cup and the J Class yacht

Yachting also seemed to have still brighter days ahead. The regatta had become a favored activity of the great English and American financiers. Cowes, on the Isle of Wight, became the world capital of yachting. Since the middle of the nineteenth century, British and American yachts have regularly competed there. The America's Cup became the ultimate prize; some have expended fortunes in pursuit of it.

In the beginning of the 1930s, the development of a new class of boat, the J Class yacht, marked a decisive turning point. Some of the most beautiful regatta yachts that have been built belong to the J Class: the *Enterprise, Rainbow, Yankee, Shamrock V* (Sir Thomas Lipton's J Class yacht), *Endeavour II* (1934), and the *Velsheda* (1933). Some of these British yachts still compete in regattas.

In addition to their role as pleasure boats, at the turn of the century, sailing ships were still used for polar exploration. Fridtjof Nansen commissioned the construction of the *Fram*. Designed by Colin Archer and launched in 1893, it later served Roald Amundsen. Robert Falcon Scott embarked on an expedition to Antarctica aboard the *Discovery*, which was launched in 1901. Between 1903 and 1910 Jean-Baptiste Charcot made several voyages of exploration aboard the *Français* and the *Pourquoi Pas?*

The Era of Sail Training

At the beginning of the twentieth century, faced with competition from steamships, sailing ships and ships powered by the combination of sail and steam were only profitable for long voyages. They were used to ship goods over great distances, such as Chilean nitrates, and wheat from San Francisco and Australia. The shipping firms of Laeisz in Germany and Erikson in Finland—the last important employers of these "Cape Horners"—used the four-masted freighters until 1939 when they brought the last shipments of Australian wheat to Europe. A period in the history of sailing was then forever ended, that of those legendary sailors who risked their lives in the perilous passage around Cape Horn in voyages through giant seas that lasted sometimes for weeks before finally the sailors found deliverance in the Pacific.

The last French Cape Horners were taken out of service between 1927 and 1933, after the passage of a law restricting the working day to eight hours. This law was fatal to the great ships, which would have had to increase their crews by 50 percent to comply with it. The only survivor of the French merchant sailing fleet was the *Laënnec*. It can be found today at Turku, Finland, where it was rechristened the *Suomen Joutsen*.

The disappearance of the Newfoundlanders

Sail-powered fishing craft lasted a little longer. At the beginning of the century, hundreds of sailing ships still embarked from the French ports of Saint-Malo and Paimpol for the fishing banks off Newfoundland. Many never returned. The last of these Newfoundland fishing boats, the *Commandant Louis Richard*, was launched by Dubigeon at

Nantes in 1934, and continued in service until 1948. Purchased by the Italian navy in 1951, it serves under the name *Palinuro*, off the coast of Sardinia, as a training ship for naval cadets. The last codfishing sailing boats to fish the banks, in 1973, were the *Creoula* and the *Argus*, both sailing under the flag of Portugal. The first still sails as a training vessel in Portugal. The second, transformed into a luxury passenger craft, today cruises the Antilles. The only other sailing ships remaining in Europe were small coastal boats. These modest sailing boats, often motorized, were found in the Baltic and the Black Seas until the end of the 1960s, when they finally fell victim to competition from mechanically powered boats. The last commercial three-masters were constructed in the 1950s in Finland, which delivered sixty wooden ships to the Soviet Union as a war reparation.

The cadets and the giants of the sea

Despite their demise as preeminent commercial vessels, however, since the beginning of the century, many have thought that great sailing ships are the best training schools for future merchant marine and naval officers. France has used boats, such as the *Borda*, to train its student officers. In the 1930s, the French naval academy ordered two "Icelandic" schooners, the *Étoile* and the *Belle Poule*, for this purpose. In the nineteenth century, Great Britain equipped the three-masted *Worcester* for naval instruction. In 1897, the Japanese converted a lightship—which had first served as the imperial yacht, launched in 1874—into a training ship, the *Meiji Maru*. The Germans, in 1901, launched the *Großherzogin Elisabeth*, a square-rigged three-master specially conceived as a sailing trainer.

Sir Philip Hunloke, at the wheel of the *Britannia* (ABOVE). The royal yacht was launched in 1892 for the future Edward VII.

The *Belle Poule* (ABOVE) and, behind, the *Étoile*.
The *Étoile* (BELOW).

The *Creole* at La Nioulargue in 1993
(ABOVE). The *Pamir* (BELOW), a four-
master that was restored in the 1950s
for both commerce and training,
tragically sank in 1957.

In the 1950s, Germany built or purchased fifteen sailing ships and fitted them out to train the cadets of both the German merchant marine and navy. Some of these vessels took on cadets while remaining commercially active. Others served exclusively as trainers. Italy, Spain, Poland, Rumania, Yugoslavia, Norway, Denmark, Belgium, and other countries followed this example and built or acquired sailing trainers. Paradoxically, the Second World War did not end this activity. While in all other domains—war, then commerce and fishing—the sailing ship had virtually disappeared, interest in sailing ships as trainers emerged in the 1950s as the last hope for the survival of great sailing vessels.

After the Second World War, Germany lost most of its pre-war fleet to the allied nations. Certain countries sold off the ships that were surrendered to them, however. Great Britain sold the *Kommodore Johnsen* (formerly the *Magdalene Vinnen*) to the Soviet Union, which rechristened it the *Sedov*. France received the *Großherzogin Elisabeth* but transformed it into a floating school under the name *Duchesse Anne*. This ship, whose rigging had been removed, was purchased and recently restored by a maritime preservation association in Dunkirk, France. The *Albert Leo Schlageter* was sent to Brazil, which commissioned it under the name *Guanabara* as a training ship for its navy. Portugal purchased it in 1962, for the same purpose, but renamed it the *Sagres II* to replace the first *Sagres*.

This movement continued, and, thanks to the efforts of associations and governments, new training ships were built for Chile, Colombia, and Ecuador; in recent years, Mexico, Poland, Japan, Russia, Great Britain, and the Netherlands have also acquired training vessels. The German maritime world did not lose its convictions with the war. Two shippers in Hamburg purchased and restored a pair of great four-masters, the *Pamir* and the *Passat*. These ships were active commercially in the 1950s, with crews of cadets in training. The tragic sinking of the *Pamir*, off the Azores in 1957, was due to an exceptionally strong hurricane and a shifting of its cargo. Most of its crew died in the disaster. The idea of fitting out large sailing ships for both training and commercial activity was then abandoned. Sailing school ships would thenceforth be fitted out exclusively for training, having fixed ballasts and rigid rules of safety. Despite the tragic loss of the *Pamir*,

the Germans completed the construction of another great sailing trainer, the *Gorch Fock II*. Many years later, other vessels were refitted as naval training ships: the *Amphitrite*, *Seute Deern II*, *Thor Heyerdahl*, and the *Alexander von Humboldt*, to name a few. The German maritime tradition was not to be abandoned easily.

Nor did yachting disappear. To the contrary, after a period of inactivity, new yachts were unveiled: the *Altaïr* in 1951; a replica of the schooner *America*, in 1967; in 1983, the *Jessica* (today the *Adix*); and others. The most beautiful of the luxury yachts launched since the end of the last century— the *Shenandoah*, *Creole*, and *Sea Cloud*, for example—have been restored.

The restoration of legendary sailing ships

Sailing ships no longer play important military or commercial roles. They can only be economically viable with the public's support. Public access is crucial to the survival of these impressive ships, and they are linked to the public in some interesting ways. Some sailing ships greet interns in sailing schools; other vessels take on passengers for luxury cruises.

Today, the world of large sailing vessels is flourishing. The International Sail Training Association, which initiated the first regatta of tall ships in 1956 between Torbay, England, and Lisbon, each year develops racing programs. The frequency of sailing races has increased from one every two years, to one, and then two, per year. As many as one hundred ships come together for these regattas. The public's enthusiasm and the rich variety of shipbuilding projects, races, and reunions demonstrate the vitality of this

ever-evolving maritime universe. Recently, a replica of a Dutch East India Company ship, the *Batavia*, was launched in the Netherlands. Numerous other projects have been initiated in recent years. Some of these are already under construction, such as Colin Mudie's design of the Indian navy's sailing trainer, the *Tarangini*, whose keel was laid in December 1995. Others are still on the drawing boards: three in Great Britain, one in Sweden, one in the Netherlands, one in New Zealand, and several in France.

The most exciting project is, without a

The *Druzhba* (ABOVE), a recently launched (1989) Russian training ship, is one of the symbols of the new dynamism of today's world of sailing ships.

The *France II* (ABOVE), the largest sailing ship ever constructed, at its launching from the Gironde shipyards at Bordeaux in 1911. The goal of the project France II–Renaissance is to see the great ship sail once again in the year 2000.

Adix (BELOW). Launched in 1983, this three-masted schooner, in the style of the great yachts of the turn of the century, is a participant in sailing's rebirth.

doubt, France's planned reconstruction of the five-masted bark, the *France II*. In 1989, Bernard Bouygues, a Frenchman from the worlds of petroleum prospecting and yachting, took note of an article by Éric Tabarly that pointed to the decay of France's maritime heritage. Bouygues was impassioned by the idea of restoring to France the great sailing ship which the nation merited. He had identified the five-masted *France II*, the largest sailing ship that the world had ever known, as the reference for the type of ship that would be worthy of reconstruction. Launched in 1913 from the Gironde shipyard in Bordeaux, to the order of the Rouen shipper Prentout-Leblond, the *France II* ran aground and sank on a reef at New Caledonia in 1922. Under Bouygues's leadership, the project of reconstructing the *France II* was born.

After four years of feasibility studies, the Association France II–Renaissance was established in 1996 with the firm support of Éric Tabarly. The first idea—the meeting of men and women committed to generating a combined one million hours of skilled work—united the industrialists, financiers,

and politicians who could assure the project's success. In purchasing hours of work through a national subscription, any citizen can participate in the financing of the reconstruction's total cost of 400 million francs. The ship, whose construction will conform to current norms of classification, will have four major missions. It will serve as an ambassador of French culture, and of the national heritage of France; as a place of apprenticeship in the national arts of maritime tourism, and as a working model of their application; and as a training school for the merchant marine, and a center for the preservation of maritime arts in general. Its activity as a cruise ship will assure its economic viability. It will accommodate two hundred passengers in double cabins. The reconstruction of the *France II* is scheduled to begin in 1998. The ship will be built in several parts, in different military and civil shipyards throughout France. The hull will be delivered and finished at Caen. The interior fittings, the engines, and the rigging will be completed in the summer of 2000. The prestigious ship will finally begin its new life in the year 2001.

Gatherings of sailing ships grow more popular each year. Tall ships set sail from Cádiz for the Columbus Race in 1992 (ABOVE RIGHT) and gather as the Freedom Armada (BELOW RIGHT) at Rouen in 1994.

The World's Great
Sailing Ships

from the *Adix* to the
Zawisza Czarny II

Adix

Then-owner of the schooner *America*, the Argentinian Carlos Perdomo, commissioned naval architect Arthur Holgate to design a three-masted schooner. Launched in 1983 from a Majorcan shipyard, the *Jessica*, as it was originally named, was the toast of yachtsmen the following summer. The magnificent sailing craft was purchased in 1990 by a British firm and rechristened the *Adix* (BELOW). Its new owners gave the yacht its present-day form. The stern was lengthened and refined, the length extended to 64.5 meters, the aft deck house removed, and the rigging simplified with the elimination of the topsail.

Alexander von Humboldt

Easily recognized by its green sails, the *Alexander von Humboldt* (RIGHT) is the training ship of the Sail Training Association Germany, the German branch of the I.S.T.A. Formerly a lightship launched in 1906, this ship was converted into a three-masted bark, measuring sixty-three meters, and began to sail in 1988. Since that time, it has taken on trainees for instruction in ocean sailing and has participated in sailing races. To facilitate maneuvers, all the yards are fixed except that of the skysail (LEFT). It has sailed to many reunions of tall ships, appearing in New York in 1992 at the celebration of the five hundredth anniversary of Christopher Columbus's arrival in America, and at Rouen in 1994.

America

In 1851, a schooner of the New York Yacht Club challenged seventeen English yachts in a regatta around the Isle of Wight. *America*, designed by George Steers and launched by the New York shipyard of William Brown, had sailed to England to participate in this race, which marked the opening of the World's Fair in London, and whose prize was a massive sterling silver trophy: the Hundred Guinea Cup. *America*'s victory that year was the origin of the prestigious sporting trial the America's Cup. In 1942, the vessel ended sadly, crushed beneath a hangar that had caved in under the weight of snow. Schaefer, the American brewer, decided to bring the celebrated vessel back to life for a promotional campaign for its beer. Relaunched in 1967, *America*, whose hull was then painted black (ABOVE), made a tour of the United States. Its exterior conformed to the original design; the interior fittings were made more functional. Its following owner, the Argentinian Carlos Perdomo, had its hull repainted white (RIGHT), which was easier to maintain in warm seas and gave the vessel the luxurious interior fittings that it presently features. Paul Deeth, one of its new owners, completely restored it in 1997, at the same time that a new replica was launched.

Amerigo Vespucci

At the prow of this ship is a figurehead representing the Italian navigator whose name has been given to both the ship and America itself. Amerigo Vespucci was the first to believe that Christopher Columbus had discovered new lands, not merely a westward ocean route to Asia. With its gilding and its stern ornamentation (RIGHT), this most prestigious of Italian warships inspires wide admiration. The *Amerigo Vespucci* (BELOW) is, nevertheless, a rather ineffectual sailing vessel. The ship must often resort to its two 950-horsepower Fiat engines; rare are the winds in which it can make headway under sail. Launched in 1931 by the former royal naval shipyard at Castellammare di Stabia, the square-rigged, three-masted vessel was designed by the Italian naval architect Francesco Rotundi. A second ship of the same type had been built three years beforehand. In 1949, it was given to the Soviet Union as a war reparation. Renamed the *Danuy*—which means "Danube" in Russian—it sailed for several years as a training ship in the Black Sea before it was decommissioned in 1963. The *Danuy* was demolished at Odessa in 1971. These two ships were built to be impressive cultural ambassadors, resembling the three-decked vessels of the mid-nineteenth century. It is true that the *Amerigo Vespucci* is first the

reflection of the prestige and distinction of the Italian navy, but it is also an important training ship. Each summer, 150 future officers of the Italian navy find their sea legs during a three-month term of instruction (RIGHT, ABOVE AND BELOW). The apprenticeship is demanding, but within a few weeks the cadets are capable, after having prepared maneuvers, of setting all sails within fifteen minutes. Nor does the commandant hesitate to order his crew to remove the upper masts when the ship, whose masts rise sixty-two meters into the air, cannot clear a

bridge to enter a port. This occurred when the *Amerigo Vespucci* voyaged to Rouen. Maneuvers are carried out in the purest tradition. Some tasks require the use of a capstan, the work being too heavy to be done by hand (NEAR RIGHT, BELOW). The sailors insert handspikes in the capstan bar-holes, in the upper part of the capstan, and push to wind the hawser.

Astrid

In 1921, the *Wuta*, a schooner built in Scheveningen in the Netherlands, began a long career as a coastal vessel. Rigged as a ketch in 1934, she was sold in 1937 to a Swede who rechristened her the *Astrid* and kept her for four decades for the transport of grain and wood. In 1957, the boat lost its masts and continued to navigate under power. In 1975, it was sold to Lebanese buyers. Stopped in the English Channel two years later by British customs officials, its crew set fire to the vessel, giving some credit to the rumors of drug trafficking. Abandoned in an English river, the *Astrid* was finally purchased by Graham Nelson, who transformed it into a brig (ABOVE) and fitted it out as a training vessel. Trainees spend terms of two to three months on board. Winters are spent in the Antilles, while summers are devoted to sailing races and gatherings such as those at Douarnenez '92 (LEFT) or Brest '96 (OPPOSITE).

Belem

The *Belem* (LEFT, BELOW) is an
antillais. When it was fitted out for
commercial activity, between its
launching in 1896 and 1913, its three
successive owners assigned it to trade
with the Antilles and Latin America.
Sold to the Duke of Westminster,
the *Belem* was extensively modified
and shone brilliantly in maritime
displays at Cannes, Cowes, and
elsewhere. In 1921, the Irish brewer
Lord Guinness became her owner

and renamed her *Fantôme II*. Between
1923 and 1924, Lord Guinness toured
the world with her, by way of
Panama and Suez. When he died in
1939, the ship was docked at the Isle
of Wight and awaited better days.
After a long tenure under the Italian
flag, the yacht *Nantais* returned to
France in 1979. Restored, it made its
inaugural voyage to New York for

the centennial of the Statue of
Liberty in 1986. Its rigging has been
restored carefully, respecting its
original form (FOLLOWING DOUBLE
PAGE). Some have criticized its
bowsprit, asserting that it is too
short (ABOVE RIGHT). Today, to
introduce people to sailing, it accepts
passengers of all ages for short
cruises along the coasts of France
(ABOVE LEFT). Such a ship demands
constant care. Its crew of nine sailors
and masters work constantly to
maintain it (LEFT, ABOVE).

Belle Étoile

Aboard strong wooden boats, sailing as far as the shores of Africa in search of rock lobster, the fishermen of Camaret, in Brittany, had long enjoyed a seafaring existence. A contest held to revive French maritime heritage inspired the idea of reconstructing a classic lobster boat.

An old hull that was disintegrating in the port, one of the last remains of a glorious age, served as the model for the project. Launched in 1992, the *Belle Étoile* (BELOW) is prized for the quality of its topsides. The vessel lives a quiet life now, taking passengers out to discover the Iroise Sea, troubled only by two attempted thefts in 1995.

Belle Poule

The *Belle Poule* and its twin sister, the *Étoile*, are the two largest sailing craft in the French navy. The two schooners are accompanied by two smaller boats, the *Mutin* and the *Grande Hermine*. The four boats appeared at Brest '96 (OPPOSITE, ABOVE). The lives of the two schooners are inextricably linked. After the French navy forsook instruction of student officers on board sailing ships, in favor of mechanized craft, at the turn of the century, advocates of sailing ceaselessly protested that instruction in sailing is the best way to develop a true sense of the sea. And it is true that no vessel allows one to feel the sea more than a sailing craft. The

finesse required to adjust sails, or the attentive skill needed to hold a steady course, provides an unmatched contact with the sea (LEFT). In contrast to navigation by motor, sailing allows a heading on only a part of the compass dial (RIGHT); a certain number of courses being impossible with any given wind. The French navy was later persuaded to build two sailing

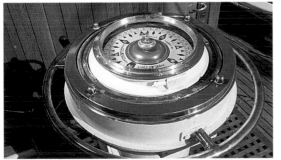

craft, based on the kind that once fished off the coast of Iceland, for the naval academy at Brest. The *Belle Poule*, launched from the shipyard at Fécamp in February 1932, was the first. Until 1940, the schooners took student officers on quick day trips or short voyages in the Iroise Sea. On June 18, 1940, several hours before the appeal of General De Gaulle, the schooners set off for England where, repainted gray, they served for a little more than five years as training vessels for British and French cadets. Returned to Brest in September 1945, their condition called for extensive repairs. It was not until 1947 that they resumed their mission as naval training craft, a mission they still assure today.

Bluenose II

In 1920, the publisher of a newspaper in Halifax organized the International Trophy of Ocean Fishermen, a regatta in which Americans and Canadians competed. The Americans won the first race. The Canadians struck back the following year with the schooner *Bluenose*, which carried off the prize and became legendary for remaining victorious until 1938. Since 1937, the Canadian ten-cent piece has proudly displayed the image of this ship. But the *Bluenose* was also a working ship whose crew sailed it to the banks. War interrupted the regatta and the proud boat was sold in 1942. Its new owners fitted the boat out for trade with the Antilles, where the ship was wrecked on a reef off Haiti in 1946. In 1963, a replica was launched from the shipyard that produced the original. After serving as a charter boat for several years, *Bluenose II* (LEFT) was purchased by the government of Nova Scotia, which remains its owner today.

Capitán Miranda

The Uruguayan ship *Capitán Miranda* carries the rigging of a modern three-masted schooner (ABOVE). This rigging is not particularly attractive, but it does allow the ship to sail closer to the wind than a square-rigged ship. The heavy super-structure, which breaks the elegant lines of the hull, was added to house the crew, the cadets in training, and any passengers that the ship might carry. Launched in 1930 in Cádiz, the ship served first as a freighter throughout South America. It lost its masts after World War II, but remained commissioned for shipping. In 1960, after a short period of inactivity, the ship was purchased by the Uruguayan government and converted for use as a hydrographic survey ship. The ship conducted detailed surveys of the coasts of Uruguay, resulting in improved nautical charts. In 1977, the government assigned the ship to the naval academy at Montevideo. Converted the following year, it makes extensive annual voyages, sailing as far as Europe.

Christian Radich

The *Christian Radich* (ABOVE) is a star of the cinema. The movie *Windjammer* was filmed on board in 1956 and 1957, during a long voyage across the Atlantic. Then, in the early 1970s, it again appeared on the screen, in the famous BBC televised series "James Onedin's Great Adventure." But the square-rigged three-master based in Oslo (RIGHT), launched from Sandefjord in 1937, is a training ship above all else. It was seized by the Germans in 1943. The Allies recovered it in 1945, in very poor condition and stripped of its masts. The ship was restored and assigned to its former mission as a training ship. Today, it prepares seventy-six young men and women each year for careers in the merchant marine.

Creole

This staysail-rigged, three-masted schooner is one of the most elegant of the classic yachts. It is shown here in 1993 at the La Nioulargue yacht gathering in Saint-Tropez (RIGHT). The crew must keep their uniforms impeccably clean, in accordance with the vessel's prestigious standing (ABOVE). The firm of Camper and Nicholsons launched the ship in 1927. It served as a naval vessel during World War II. From 1951 until 1978, its Greek owner lived and worked on board. In 1956, the *Creole* participated in the first race of tall ships. Renamed the *Mistral* under the Danish flag, she participated in two legs of the 1980 race. When Maurizio Gucci bought her in 1983, her name was restored.

Cauauhtémoc

The three-masted Mexican ship *Cuauhtémoc* (TOP) was built in Bilbao in 1982. It was the last of four sailing ships—along with the *Gloria*, the *Guayas*, and the *Simon Bolivar*—ordered by Latin American countries from the same shipyard since 1967. It accepts cadets (ABOVE RIGHT) from various schools of the Mexican navy. The ship visited Japan in 1983, Tahiti in 1984 and 1987, Europe in 1985, and the Mediterranean in 1988. In the course of its circumnavigation of the globe in 1990, it voyaged 26,785 miles in 180 days. The *Cuauhtémoc* won its laurels as a Cape Horner in a journey around South America in 1992–93, after having participated in the Columbus Race. It was present at the gatherings of tall ships in Rouen in 1989 and 1994 (LEFT). Twenty-eight officers (ABOVE LEFT), forty-eight petty officers, and a crew of fifty-two men and 116 cadets live on board. The ship's name, *Cuauhtémoc*, meaning "the eagle which descends," is the name of the last Aztec emperor, whose figure is mounted on the prow. To Mexicans, *Cuauhtémoc* represents the virtues of courage and willingness to sacrifice for one's country. As ambassador of the Mexican nation, the *Cuauhtémoc* is fitted with handsome reception salons (FOLLOWING DOUBLE PAGE).

Danmark

In early 1929, the five-masted training ship *København* mysteriously disappeared with seventy-five passengers during a voyage from Montevideo to Australia. Subsequently, the four-masted *Viking* was sold to the Erikson shipyard in Mariehamn on Finland's Åland islands, for the grain trade

with Australia. As a result, Denmark had no sailing ship trainer at its disposal. The government decided to build a square-rigged three-master for use in training the cadets of the Danish merchant marine. Launched in 1932, the *Danmark* (ABOVE) can accommodate 120 cadets. The ship was docked in New York in 1939, where it was participating in the World's Fair, when it was surprised by the outbreak of war in Europe. Its commander, Knud Hansen, received orders to remain in the United States. When the Americans entered the war in 1941, the vessel was placed at the disposal of the United States Coast Guard Academy. Through 1945, five thousand cadets were trained on the ship. After the *Danmark* returned to Europe, the success of its mission with the Coast Guard persuaded American authorities to pursue the same training with the *Horst Wessel*, which was rechristened the *Eagle*. In 1959, the number of cadets accepted was reduced to eighty, with sixteen crew members. Today, the vessel accepts two classes of apprentices for terms of five months, and regularly makes Atlantic crossings. It was present in 1986 at the centennial of the Statue of Liberty (PRECEDING DOUBLE PAGE).

Dar Mlodziezy

At the end of the 1970s, Poland dreamed of renewing its fleet of tall ship training schools. Among others, the *Dar Pomorza* had come to the end of its career. Zygmunt Choren, a young naval architect bursting with revolutionary ideas, was commissioned to draw up plans for its replacement. The *Dar Mlodziezy* (OPPOSITE RIGHT, ABOVE) emerged from the naval shipyards in Gdansk in 1981. The bridge is located at the spar deck; that is to say, the poop and the forecastle decks have been eliminated. The yards are stationary. In order to provide for interior space, Choren conceived a surprising squared stern. The modern design of the hull per-

mits an improved performance, and the three-master handles very well in rough weather. Here it is seen running close to the wind on a starboard tack in a choppy sea (BELOW). Despite the apparently simplified design of the rigging, work on the ship remains very demanding (RIGHT, BELOW). In 1982, the *Dar Pomorza* finally returned to its dock at Gdansk, where it was transformed into a museum, while the *Dar Mlodziezy*, whose name means "gift of youth," voyages across the oceans of the earth. It rounded Cape Horn under sail in 1988, in the course of a two-year circumnavigation of the globe.

Eagle

The *Eagle*, the three-masted trainer of the United States Coast Guard, is easily recognized by the red and blue diagonal stripes painted on its hull (RIGHT MIDDLE). It carries a magnificent prow figure representing an American bald eagle, the emblem of the United States from which the ship has taken its name (RIGHT, ABOVE). At the end of World War II, strengthened through the training experience aboard the *Danmark*, the Coast Guard decided to commission for the same mission—the training of future Coast Guard officers—a vessel received from Germany as war reparation, the *Horst Wessel*, which was renamed the *Eagle*. This boat today trains 150 men and women each year, regularly undertaking long voyages to Europe. It sailed to Rouen in 1989 (ABOVE) and in 1994. The *Horst Wessel* was launched at Hamburg in 1936 by Blohm & Voß for the German navy. Its design, like that of the *Sagres II*, the *Mircea*, and the *Gorch Fock II*, was inspired by the *Gorch Fock*, which was launched in 1933 and

today is known as the *Tovarishch*. The *Eagle*'s rigging has been slightly modified by the Americans, who removed its double spanker (RIGHT, BELOW). Discipline aboard is rigorous, but the result is a widely respected training. *Eagle Seamanship, a Manual for Square-Rigger Sailing* is the work of reference for sailors who work with square-rigging.

Endeavour

Among the most famous of the J Class yachts, the *Endeavour* (ABOVE, AND RIGHT) was launched in 1934 and today navigates along the east coast of the United States, offering its luxurious accommodations to passengers. The unhappy challenger for the America's Cup in 1934, opposing Thomas Sopwith's American yacht the *Rainbow*, it has nevertheless a proud record of victory in many regattas. Its successor, *Endeavour II*, had no more success and was demolished before World War II. After the war, the *Endeavour* served as a residence. Purchased by an English foundation, and moored at Cowes, the J Class yacht awaited restoration for many years. It was finally purchased and restored by Elizabeth Meyer, who is still the owner.

Esmeralda

In 1946, the keel of a tall ship was laid at Cádiz. The new vessel was to be built following the same plans as the *Juan Sebastían de Elcano* and was to replace this ship, which was then judged to be too old. However, following a serious fire that partially destroyed the boat, the work was abandoned. Work was resumed in 1952 and the ship was launched the following year. At that time it was named the *Juan de Austria*. During this same period, Spain was in dispute with Chile, which had supplied Spain with enormous quantities of salt-peter for the manufacture of munitions. Chile called for the settlement of the debt that Spain had not honored. The Spanish government proposed to offer the newly built vessel in exchange for the retirement

of its debt. The government of Chile promptly accepted. The tall ship was delivered in 1954 to the Chileans, who made some modifications to it. They installed the rigging of a four-masted schooner and extended the forecastle. They also increased the sail spread by installing three large balloon jibs between the masts. Rechristened the *Esmeralda* (ABOVE, AND LEFT), and based at Valparaíso, the ship went into service in September 1954. It has since circumnavigated the world several times, accepting from fifty to ninety cadets each year. When calling on London, the crew of the ship did not hesitate to remove some ballast to be able to sail up the Thames. The ship participated in the Columbus Race in 1992. Photographed during the race, it is here preceded by the *Dar Mlodziezy* (FOLLOWING DOUBLE PAGE).

Étoile

The *Étoile* (LEFT, AND BELOW) is the twin sister of the *Belle Poule*. The second sailing ship built for the naval academy in Brest, it was launched in July 1932. The blueprints of the two sister ships were based on the schooners that had fished off Iceland between 1832 and 1935. The navy yard at Fécamp, in Normandy, under the direction of Mr. Chantelot and Mr. Lemaistre, was chosen for its reputation as a builder of excellent sail-powered fishing boats. The exterior lines of these boats are more elegant than those of the Icelandic fishing craft that served as their models, and their interior fittings were modified to accommodate thirty student-officers and an engine. The underside of the ship was sheathed with copper. The rigging included a remarkable feature, a roller-furling topsail (LEFT). This square sail, rigged to a yard on the mizzenmast, could be pulled in from the bridge by means of an ingenious system. Instead of being rolled by hand by men who had climbed up to it through the rigging, the sail is roller-furled around a spar placed just below the yardarm and controlled from the deck. Some details distinguish the *Belle Poule* from the *Étoile*. The fairleads of the first are painted black; those of the latter are painted white. The reverse is true of the trucks of their mainmasts: the *Belle Poule*'s mainmast truck is white, while that of the *Étoile* is black.

Étoile Molène

In 1994, in the midst of the most modern tall ships, an old craft set off on the Rhum race. Bob Escoffier was alone at the helm of his distinctive orange-and-white-sailed vessel, the

Étoile Molène, the only craft with fore and aft rigging. Built by the famous ship's carpenter Auguste Tertu, this ketch was launched in 1954 in Fret, near Brest. Christened the *Étoile*, in its debut fishing season it escaped a terrible storm in which several other vessels disappeared. It alternately fished for tuna in the Bay of Biscay and trawled off Iceland. Decommissioned at the port of Douarnenez in the early 1980s, the abandoned vessel sank a few years later. It was brought to the surface, but was left unrestored. When Bob Escoffier acquired the boat in 1990, its condition required extensive work. With the experience and knowledge that he had acquired in the restoration of his first boat, the ketch *Popoff*, the task did not daunt him. The result was impressive (ABOVE, AND LEFT). He can now carry twenty passengers in exceptional comfort. The *Étoile Molène* was at Brest '92 and Brest '96. In 1994, the vessel, equipped with winches to facilitate maneuvering, set off on the transatlantic crossing. Bob was forced to fall back on the Azores, however, but afterward managed to continue on to the Antilles.

Europa

A former lightship that was transformed into a three-masted bark, *Europa* is one of the rare ships to carry studding sails (ABOVE). The square studding sail is a supplementary sail rigged on a boom extending from the yardarm. Here, the crew has set, from bottom to top, a lower studding sail, a topmast studding sail, and a topgallant studding sail. The ship, launched in 1911 as the *Senator Brockes*, sails today under the Dutch flag and offers cruises along the coasts of Northern Europe.

Eye of the Wind

Eye of the Wind is certainly among the most beautiful sailing ships, as was attested when it was awarded the Prix d'Élégance in 1994. It has circled the world several times and has participated in many yacht races and gatherings of sailing ships from the Pacific to Europe and the United States. In 1992, the brown-sailed bark schooner was found at the start of the Columbus Race. With squared yards, it is here shown in brisk pursuit of the *Cuauhtémoc* (FOLLOWING DOUBLE PAGE). Like the *Europa*, it was launched in

Germany in 1911. *Eye of the Wind* served first as a merchant ship between Europe and South America. Then, sold to a Swedish owner, it was refitted to haul freight during the winter and to fish during the summer. It lost its masts in the 1950s. Ravaged by a fire in 1969, it was saved in 1973, when a group of sailing enthusiasts began its restoration. In the early 1980s, it appeared in several feature films. It was during these years that the ship's rigging was altered to its present form, a topsail bark schooner. *Eye of the Wind* won honors as a Cape Horner in 1991.

Falken

Until 1938, the Swedish navy had at its disposal two three-masted square-riggers for the instruction of adolescents between the ages of thirteen and fifteen. The *Najaden* and the *Jarramas* were decommissioned in 1938 and 1946, respectively. The first of these ships was transformed into a museum in the city of Halmstad; the second ship became a museum and restaurant in Karlskrona. Launched in 1946 and 1947, respectively, the *Gladan* and the *Falken* replaced them. These two elegant schooners, whose design was inspired by the German pilot boats of the North Sea, can rig a square cross-jack sail, as seen in this view of the *Falken* with the crew at work on the yardarm (LEFT). For a number of years now, budget cuts and the limited number of cadets has led to the decommissioning of one or the other schooner in alternate years.

Fryderyk Chopin

The *Fryderyk Chopin* is a modern fifty-five-meter sailing ship. Its architect, Zygmunt Choren, the designer of the *Pogoria* and the *Dar Mlodziezy*, envisioned a bark—a ship that requires a sizable crew to maneuver. It was for this reason that the more complicated rigging was abandoned, although such rigging would have had the virtue of occupying the numerous young trainees aboard the Polish sailing ship. It is a solid craft, as shown in this view taken during a gust of wind before its participation in the Columbus Race (RIGHT). The *Fryderyk Chopin*, which was recently built and was launched in 1992, has already sailed many miles. In addition to its voyages to the United States, South Africa, and Brazil, it has also cruised the Mediterranean, and winters in the Antilles, the Canaries, or the Azores.

Georg Stage II

In 1882, a Danish shipper, Frederyk Stage, established a foundation to which he gave the name of his son, Georg Stage, who had died prematurely at the age of twenty-two. A square-rigged three-master, the *Georg Stage* was built in 1882 and served until 1934 as a training ship for young cadets of the Danish merchant marine. Judged to be too old for training purposes, the ship was then sold to the celebrated writer Alan John Villiers, who renamed it the *Joseph Conrad*. In the years that followed, it sailed some fifty-eight thousand miles around the world. In 1937, Villiers published a book that recounted the ship's adventures, titled *The Voyage of the Conrad*. Since 1948, the ship has been preserved in the United States at the Mystic Seaport Museum. As for the Danish foundation, it commissioned a Danish shipyard in Frederykshavn to build a new, small, square-rigged three-master. Launched in 1934, the *Georg Stage II* (RIGHT) measures fifty-two meters from stem to stern. With a regular crew of thirteen, since 1981 the ship has accepted eighty boys and girls between the ages of fifteen and eighteen. The young people sleep in hammocks. For six months of each year, the ship makes a number of short voyages, for the most part in the Baltic and the North Sea. The young cadets embark at Copenhagen, a month before the first voyage, to prepare the vessel. It is the cadets who reset the sails and who prepare the running rigging for the voyage. They also lay up the sails and rigging at the end of the season. From time to time, the ship makes more important tours. In 1989, it rallied for the first time to the United States. It is today the sailing ship whose profile most closely resembles that of the classic merchant ships of the nineteenth century.

Gloria

Nearly two thousand cadets have trained on the *Gloria* over the past thirty years (RIGHT). The sailing ship, launched in 1967, is a school that trains the future officers of the Colombian navy (OPPOSITE). It is also, and perhaps primarily, a prestigious ambassador for its country, charged to promote not only the nation in general, but also its industry, its trade, and its tourism. The *Gloria* helps educate the public about its nation with the aid of an exhibit area, installed on board in 1975, that presents the economic, geographic, and cultural heritage of Colombia. The ship participates in numerous international events and tall ship races, such as Opsail in New York in 1976, the Columbus Race in 1992, and the reunions held in Rouen in 1989 and 1994 (FOLLOWING DOUBLE PAGE). Note, in the photographs on the following pages, the shell plate that reflects the sun's brightness. The *Gloria* voyages often. It has called on almost sixty countries on five continents. In 1970, it circumnavigated the globe, visiting Venezuela, Brazil, Argentina, South Africa, Australia, New Zealand, Chile, and Ecuador, whose navy is the owner of a ship, the *Guayas*, which was launched in 1978 from the same shipyard that produced the *Gloria*. The cadets live together in a large central battery deck where they sleep by night and receive instruction by day.

Gorch Fock II

Germany's tradition of training its sailors reaches back into the nineteenth century. Certain tall ships were designed exclusively to serve as sailing schools. Others, fitted out for commerce, also took on cadets. Despite the breakup of the German association's fleet after the Second World War, the Germans have proved loyal to this tradition. Schliewen, a Hamburg shipowner, saved the *Pamir* and the *Passat* from demolition in Belgium in 1951. These two four-masted ships had belonged to Laeisz, the German shipping company. Beginning in 1954, both sailed again as commercial vessels and received cadets as well. The German

navy then decided to replace its pre-war school ships, the *Gorch Fock*, the *Horst Wessel*, and the *Albert Leo Schlageter*—surrendered in 1945 as war reparations to the Soviets and the Americans—with a new three-master built according to the same plans. The sinking in September 1957 of the *Pamir*, which took eighty-six persons down with her, did not interrupt this work, but pressured the German navy to follow even more stringent safety measures. The *Gorch Fock II* was finally launched in 1958 (RIGHT). A regular participant in tall ship races, where the precision of its maneuvers inspires admiration (ABOVE), it is also present at many reunions, such as those in Rouen in 1989 and 1994 (OPPOSITE).

HMS Rose

The *HMS Rose* (ABOVE) is a replica of an eighteenth-century warship. Its masts carry full topsails and full topgallants (LEFT, AND OPPOSITE). These sails are very large and can be a handicap. The topmen have the delicate job of scrambling up the masts to reef them in, when the weather calls for a shortening of sail. This arrangement also limits the possibilites of coming into the wind. The original *HMS Rose*, launched in 1757, was an English frigate that fought the French in Europe and in the Antilles, and later was engaged against the colonists in the American War of Independence. Its career was ended when it was scuttled in the Savannah River, in Georgia, to block the passage of a French fleet that had come to the aid of the besieged

Americans. In 1970, the Canadian shipyard Smith & Rhuland was commissioned to reconstruct the *Rose*. The original plans of Hugh Blades had been unearthed at the National Maritime Museum in Greenwich, England. Originally unequipped for sailing, the *Rose* served for ten years as a dockside attraction in Newport, Rhode Island. Repurchased and fitted to conform to the rigorous United States Coast Guard regulations that apply to passenger ships, the *Rose* now puts out to sea along the coasts of the United States and in the Great Lakes, offering short voyages of instruction. But the *Rose* has also made long voyages, such as its transatlantic passage to Europe for the reunions at Bristol '96 and Brest '96. Such gatherings provided occasions for the crew to fire the artillery, which is installed on the top and battery decks.

Jens Krogh

The *Jens Krogh*, a Danish twenty-one-meter, ketch-rigged sailing trainer, was launched in 1899. It was commissioned by P. Møller, a commercial fisherman of Frederikshavn, from a shipyard of the same town. Its hull enclosed a tank that conserved fish until they were delivered to port by another boat especially built for that purpose. From the beginning, the *Jens Krogh* was also equipped with a gasoline engine. It continued its career as a fishing boat until 1973, although by that time it had lost a part of its rigging. An association at Ålborg purchased the boat and restored it. Given its original name, it was refitted with its original rigging, made up of three head sails, a mainsail, a gaff sail, and a mizzen (BELOW). The fish tank was fitted out as living quarters for nineteen trainees. The sailboat was finally ready for its relaunch in 1977. It sails along the Danish coast, but devotes the summer to tall ship races. It voyaged to America in 1992 to participate in the Columbus Race.

Juan Sebastián de Elcano

Launched in 1927 in Cádiz, the *Juan Sebastián de Elcano* is a four-masted schooner (RIGHT). Its mizzenmast carries three topsails and can carry a square cross-jack. In addition to gaff sails, the crew can set top staysails between each mast. The ship took the name of the officer who assumed command of the expedition of Magellan after he was killed in the Philippines. He was the first mariner, with the eighteen men of his crew, to achieve a circumnavigation of the globe. The Spanish training ship has since proved itself worthy of its name, for it has circled the globe seven times. Today, it receives eighty-nine cadets with its regular crew of 243 officers and crew members. In 1976, the vessel attended the U.S. bicentennial celebration in New York. Shortly before, it had collided with an Argentinian ship, the *Libertad*, whose bowsprit became entangled in the back stays of its topmast. In 1992, the *Juan Sebastián de Elcano* served as the flagship of the fleet that gathered for the Columbus Race.

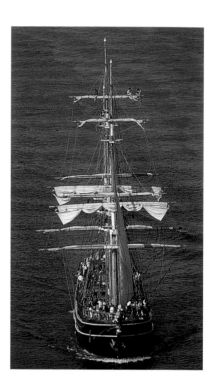

Kaiwo Maru II

Training sailors on tall ships has enjoyed a long tradition in Japan. In 1897, the Japanese government converted the *Meiji Maru*—a former imperial yacht constructed in Scotland in 1874—into a square-rigged, three-masted training ship. In 1909, the Japanese constructed another training ship, the *Unyo Maru*. Two 110-meter four-masted barks were launched in 1930 at Kobe.

Commissioned as training ships for merchant marine cadets, these ships, the *Nippon Maru* and the *Kaiwo Maru*, were replaced, respectively, in 1984 and 1989 by sailing ships carrying the same names. They vary from their predecessors only in some details, such as the more modern shape of their anchors. The *Kaiwo Maru II* (ABOVE) rarely leaves the Pacific. Nevertheless, it has occasionally voyaged to New York, as shown here, in 1992 (PRECEDING DOUBLE PAGE).

Kaskelot

Originally, the *Kaskelot* (ABOVE, AND RIGHT) was a freight vessel designed to navigate in the icy waters off Greenland. The Danish shipyard J. Ring Andersen launched this strong, ketch-rigged wooden ship in 1948. It was endowed with a double-hull, whose sides were up to ten centimeters thick. Commissioned by the Royal Greenland Company, the ship was assigned to transport supplies. Its name, *kaskelot*, means "sperm-whale" in Danish. In 1993, Robin Davis purchased it and transformed it into a three-masted bark for the filming of movies. In 1984, it returned to Greenland to appear in the drama *Terra Nova* about Robert Falcon Scott's expeditions. It also made an appearance in the French film *Beaumarchais l'Insolent* in 1995 and the French television series "La Rivière Espérance," which was filmed off Cherbourg.

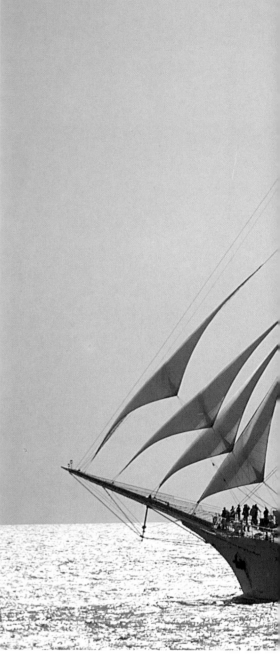

Khersones

The *Khersones* (ABOVE, AND LEFT) was commissioned to replace the *Tovarishch* when, in the 1980s, the Soviets wanted to renew their fleet of tall ship trainers. This square-rigged three-master was constructed in the shipyard in Gdansk following the plans that were used to build the *Dar Mlodziezy*, whose performance so impressed the Soviet authorities that they felt compelled to order a new fleet. Launched in 1989, it was one of

a series of five of the same type. Based in Kerch, on the Black Sea, it went immediately into service for training of merchant marine cadets (RIGHT). In 1991, it began to take passengers from the West. Difficulties accumulated after 1993, when the ship passed under the Ukrainian flag. The crew was no longer paid, and the maintenance and resupply of the boat became problematic. The situation has since improved. In January 1997, the *Khersones* rounded Cape Horn with one hundred Western passengers.

Kruzenshtern

Until 1939, shipping magnate
F. Laeisz remained one of the world's
last owners of tall ship merchant
vessels. His fleet was called the "Flying P. Line" because of his adopted
the practice of giving to all his ships
names beginning with the letter "P."
Only in the case of the *Henriette Vehn*
was this tradition not upheld. However, in the rash of confiscation after
World War I, most of his fleet was
taken from him. But Laeisz was not a
man to accept defeat. He repurchased
some of his ships and commissioned
others to be built. On June 24, 1926,
a new four-masted ship was launched,
the *Padua*, known today as the *Kruzenshtern* (ABOVE). From the beginning, its quarters were fitted out to
accommodate cadets. The ship's first
voyages led it by way of Cape Horn
to Talcahuano, Chile, where it picked

up a cargo of nitrates. It lost four
men to violent winds off Cape Horn
in 1930, during its return to Europe.
In 1933, it was assigned to transport
grain shipments between Australia
and Europe and participated in the
famous wheat races. The *Kruzenshtern*
circumnavigated the world in 1939,
when it sailed from Hamburg to
Valparaíso by way of Cape Horn,
before it set a course for Port
Lincoln, Australia, where it took on a
load of wheat. It participated with
thirteen tall ships in the last race that
year. Requisitioned by the German
navy, it served as a training ship and
remained confined to the Baltic Sea
throughout the war. Russians seized
it in 1946 in Svinemünde and gave it
the name of a nineteenth-century
Russian explorer, Adam Johann von
Kruzenshtern. But it was only in 1959
that a refurbishing of the *Kruzenshtern*
got under way. In 1961, it was

assigned with the *Sedov* to
hydrographic and oceanographic
research duty in the Atlantic and the
Mediterranean. The Soviet government then assigned it, in 1965, to the
ministry of fishing. The ship was
employed after that time as a training
vessel for cadets of the fisheries
schools, who took some of their
lessons in the immense rigging
(FOLLOWING DOUBLE PAGE) of the four-
masted bark, one of the world's largest
sailing ships. In 1990, the Soviets
opened it to Western students. After
the breakup of the Soviet Union, it
sailed under the Russian flag. Subsequently, it was decommissioned, and
was used briefly in Germany as a
youth hostel. The *Kruzenshtern* sails
again, thanks to German funds that
financed its restoration in 1994. Since
its first participation in a race of tall
ships in 1974, it has been present at all
the great reunions (LEFT).

La Cancalaise

At the turn of the century, solid working boats, trimmed with vast spreads of canvas, cut through the waters of the Bay of Mont-Saint-Michel. There, fishermen dragged oysters, bottom fished, and trawled. These vessels were the *bisquines*, or fishing smacks, whose rigging shared something in common with that of the coasting lugger: three masts, two of which could be rigged for three sails. When fishing, the crews set two sails on the mizzenmast and two on the mainmast, with the lowermost

sail set on the jiggermast, as shown here on *La Cancalaise* (ABOVE). During a regatta, a third sail could be added to each mast. The golden age of this craft lasted from the end of the nineteenth century until the 1920s, although the owners of the bisquines continued to race each other until the beginning of the Second World War. In the 1950s, Jean Le Bot, refusing to allow this precious heritage to disappear, redrew the plans of one of these sailing craft. Le Bot's model was *La Perle*, whose many regatta victories over its arch rivals from Granville had made it the pride of

the Cancalais. Impressed by the public interest in France's maritime heritage, the citizens of Cancale decided in the mid-1980s to renew their connection with their port's rich past. A new bisquine, *La Cancalaise*, was built from the plans of *La Perle*, and was launched in April 1987. The new crew discovered the sailing lore of bygone days, thanks to the old sailors who had worked the bisquines. *La Cancalaise* has since participated in many gatherings and regattas, such as the Cross Channel Race of the Old Raffiots. Here, the boat is photographed in front of the *Pride of Baltimore* at Brest '96 (RIGHT).

La Granvillaise

The launch of *La Cancalaise* demanded a response from the citizens of Granville. In addition to their talents for oyster dragging and trawling, the bisquines of Granville had been quite famous for their success in bottom fishing. Why didn't the Norman port also have its own bisquine? The shipyard set to work in December 1988 and *La Granvillaise* (LEFT) was launched in April 1990. To distinguish the ship from its Breton sister, its hull was painted white and decorated with a sheer rail painted green. It measured nineteen meters in length and required thirty-two meters of docking space. The two bisquines eagerly renewed the pre-war racing tradition and met for a regatta. *La Granvillaise* lost one of its masts at one of the very first of these meetings, but this only delayed the match. In 1996, during the competition between the fishing ports, skipper Isabelle Autissier led the Norman bisquine to victory over *La Cancalaise*, which was captained by Christophe Augin.

La Recouvrance

In 1988, the magazine *Le Chasse-Marée* (*Coasting Lugger*) launched a competition called "Boats of the Coasts of France," to encourage each French port to reconstruct a boat representative of its history. The city of Brest, which in 1992 was to preside over this, the largest gathering of old sailing ships ever organized in France—and was also to judge the competition—had to have its own boat to show. It chose to reconstruct a nineteenth-century war schooner. The sailing ship was christened *La Recouvrance*, after the name of a section of the city. The Guip shipyard laid the ship's keel in April 1991. Its launching on July 14, 1992, was regarded as the highpoint of Brest '92. While the Guip shipyard slowly completed the interior fitting of the ship, *La Recouvrance* ran several trials in the Iroise Sea (RIGHT, ABOVE, AND FOLLOWING DOUBLE PAGE) and

made its first voyage to La Rochelle (RIGHT, BELOW). In 1995, it represented its home port at a yacht gathering in Amsterdam. In the course of its voyage, it lost its bowsprit boom and its topmast. The ship sailed to Bristol in May 1996 and was the star at Brest '96, where it first competed in a regatta against its great American rival, the *Pride of Baltimore II*.

Britain in 1898, decommissioned in 1954, and transformed into a museum at Buenos Aires. The keel of the *Libertad* was laid in 1953 and its hull launched in 1956, but the ship did not enter into service until 1960. Its inaugural voyage in 1963 lasted six months and took the ship to Europe. It called on Lisbon, Le Havre, and Hamburg, where it received thirty thousand visitors. In 1966, it beat the speed record for a transatlantic crossing between Canada and Great Britain, with an average speed of 10.5 knots and peak speeds of 18 knots. In 1964, the *Libertad* participated in the Lisbon-Bermuda race, then in Operation Sail, in New York. It also took part in each of the races organized for the tall ships: in 1976; in 1983, on the occasion of the 450th anniversary of Jacques Cartier's landing in Canada; and in 1992, at the Columbus Race. Its training

Libertad

An Argentinian military training ship, the *Libertad* (LEFT, ABOVE, AND FOLLOWING DOUBLE PAGE) is one of the world's largest sailing vessels. It measures 105 meters from stem to stern. Its long bowsprit makes it possible to rig four jib sails in addition to the storm jib, whose stay is attached to the deck (BELOW). The ship was built to replace the *Presidente Sarmiento*, a square-rigged three-master that was launched in Great

voyages with the cadets of the Rio Santiago Naval Academy often take it to Europe. For example, the *Libertad* called on London in 1975, 1979, and for the last time in 1981 (the following year Argentina and Great Britain went to war over the Falkland Islands). It also appeared at the Sails of Freedom, at Rouen in 1989, on the occasion of the bicentennial of the French Revolution. The figure on its prow, a representation of liberty, was the symbol of that celebration (ABOVE).

Malcom Miller

The Sail Training International Race Committee was established in Great Britain in 1954 to organize races of the tall ship sailing schools. Renamed the Sail Training Association in June 1956, it organized in July of that year a race between Torbay, England, and Lisbon, Portugal. The organization's growth in the 1960s allowed it to acquire its own training ship, the *Sir Winston Churchill*, a three-masted schooner which was launched in 1966. Shortly afterward, Sir James Miller, the mayor of Edinburgh, offered to pay half the cost of the construction of a new ship, under the condition that it be named the *Malcom Miller* (ABOVE, AND LEFT), in homage to his son, who had died the year before in an automobile accident. The ship was built following the blueprints of the *Sir Winston Churchill* and was launched in 1968. Beginning in 1972, it embarked on some training missions with crews entirely composed of women. The first ship, the *Sir Winston Churchill*, won a leg of the sailing race in that year. Today, in light of the success of the first two boats, the S.T.A. is planning the construction of a third vessel.

Maria Asumpta

Until recently the *Maria Assumpta* (RIGHT) was the world's oldest active sailing ship. Built in Ibiza in 1858, this old coastal vessel was impressively restored. About to be destroyed, it was purchased in 1980 by two Englishmen, already the owners of the *Marques*, for the filming of a movie. But the film project ended suddenly, and the ship took on trainees. Overturned by a violent blast of wind in the Bermudas in 1984, the *Marques* went under, taking nineteen passengers with her. The *Maria Assumpta* continued sailing, voyaging to Douarnezez in 1992 (ABOVE). On May 30, 1995, driven toward the coast by the strong currents at Rumps Point, in Cornwall, the brig's motor failed and the vessel broke apart on the rocks. Three passengers perished.

Mariette

This elegant schooner, the *Mariette* (ABOVE LEFT), was launched in 1916 from a Rhode Island shipyard. It was designed by the famous American naval architect, Nathanael Greene Herreshoff, the visionary behind many of the yachts that defended the America's Cup at the turn of the century. Its first owner was a Boston industrialist, Frederick Brown. It was purchased in 1927 by Keno Crown-inshield, who gave it the name *Cleopatra's Barge II.* Caught up in the Second World War, it was requisitioned by the United States Coast Guard. It was returned to its owner in 1946, but judging it in too poor condition, he put it up for sale. In the 1950s, the schooner crossed the Pacific Ocean under the name *Gee Gee.* It had been converted into a charter boat in the Antilles when Walter Boudreau purchased it and renamed it the *Janeen.* Sold to an Italian owner in 1979, it has been meticulously restored, as can be seen in the details of its boom and its compass housing (ABOVE RIGHT, TOP AND BOTTOM).

Mir

Launched in 1987, the *Mir* is the first of the five tall ships built on the model of the *Dar Mlodziezy* and delivered to the Soviet Union between 1987 and 1991. Painted white, it can be distinguished from its elder by a smaller spanker sail and by the color of its masts. In this aerial view, its spar deck is clearly visible (LEFT). Based in Saint Petersburg, the *Mir* trains the cadets of the College of Naval Mechanics. Opened in 1991 to Western trainees, it participates regularly in tall ship races. Important modifications made at a German shipyard in 1992 included the installation of a stem propeller and the remodeling of several cabins to make them more comfortable for Western passengers. It participated that summer in the Columbus Race. On numerous occasions, the *Mir*, called "the world's fastest training ship," has demonstrated its prowess in tall ship races.

Notre Dame de Rumengol

The high point of the Brest '96 gathering was the July 14 relaunching of the *Notre Dame de Rumengal*, which had just received a complete refurbishing (ABOVE). This ketch-rigged sailing barge built of wood and steel was launched on July 15, 1945. Beginning an international career the following year, it set off for Oran, Algeria, to take on a cargo of wine destined for ports in southern France. It was then assigned to transport onions, cauliflower, and strawberries between Plougastel, France, and Portsmouth, England. From 1955, the sailing vessel was active in harvesting sand from the roadstead of Brest and the Iroise Sea for use in construction and land improvement. Its ninety-eight-horsepower motor served it well, both to propel the boat when necessary and to rotate the winding drum that hauled its dredging bucket. Decommissioned in 1981, it was purchased by an association which restored it between 1984 and 1989. Again fit for navigation, it was classed as a historic monument in 1991. Exhibitions of local history are often displayed in its immense hold.

Oosterschelde

Launched from a Dutch shipyard in 1918, the *Oosterschelde* (LEFT, AND BELOW) was first assigned as a merchant vessel to ship cargoes of brick, salted herring, grain, straw, and bananas between northern Europe, Africa, and the Mediterranean. Its rigging was reduced in 1930, and, in 1939, it passed from Dutch hands into Danish ownership, whereupon the vessel was renamed the *Fulgen*. It navigated the Baltic and over routes that took it to Ireland, Spain, France, Italy, and Tunisia. The *Fulgen* was purchased in 1953 by a Swede, Sam Peterson, who rechristened it the *Sylvan* and used it as a coastal vessel in the Baltic. In 1961 and 1962, the boat underwent modernization that rendered it unrecognizable. In 1967, the coastal ship returned to the Dutch flag, but it was not until 1988 that Dick van Andel stepped forward to acquire it. He restored its original name and envisioned returning it to its original condition. After patient research and a long period of restoration, the ship was relaunched in 1992. A magnificent salon, equipped with a fireplace, a library, a piano, and a bar (ABOVE), had been installed in the ship's ancient hold. The following year, the *Oosterschelde* took part in a tall ship race in the North Sea. But its owner's dream was to sail it around the world. The ship left Europe in October 1996 for Hong Kong, from which it set out in a race for Japan, returning by way of Cape Horn after an adventurous detour to Antarctica.

Palinuro

Since the sixteenth century, sailing ships throughout Europe have fished for cod off the banks of Newfoundland. One of the principal French ports for the Newfoundlanders was Saint-Malo, a city of pirates and privateers. In the beginning of the century, Saint-Malo sent scores of wooden ships across the Atlantic to Newfoundland each year. At the beginning of the 1930s, Joseph Briand, who had aggressively established himself in the codfishing business, broke tradition and commissioned a pair of fifty-four-meter steel schooners from the Dubigeon shipyard in Nantes; the prevailing practice was to build such ships in wood.

In fact, it was only the second time that a sailing ship in steel had been ordered for fishing the banks. The *Commandant Louis Richard* and the *Lieutenant René Guillon* were launched in 1934. Ruined by their costly construction, Briand was forced to sell the vessels immediately. The Labrador fisheries under the direction of Mr. Glâtre purchased them. Until 1948, the *Commandant Louis Richard* voyaged each year to fish the Newfoundland banks. Sold once again, the ship sailed twice as a freighter to the Indian Ocean under the name the *Jean Marc Aline*. Considered by the French merchant marine for training, it was finally sold to the Italian navy in 1951 and renamed the *Palinuro* (RIGHT). Today based at La Maddalena, in Sardinia (ABOVE), it rarely leaves the Mediterranean.

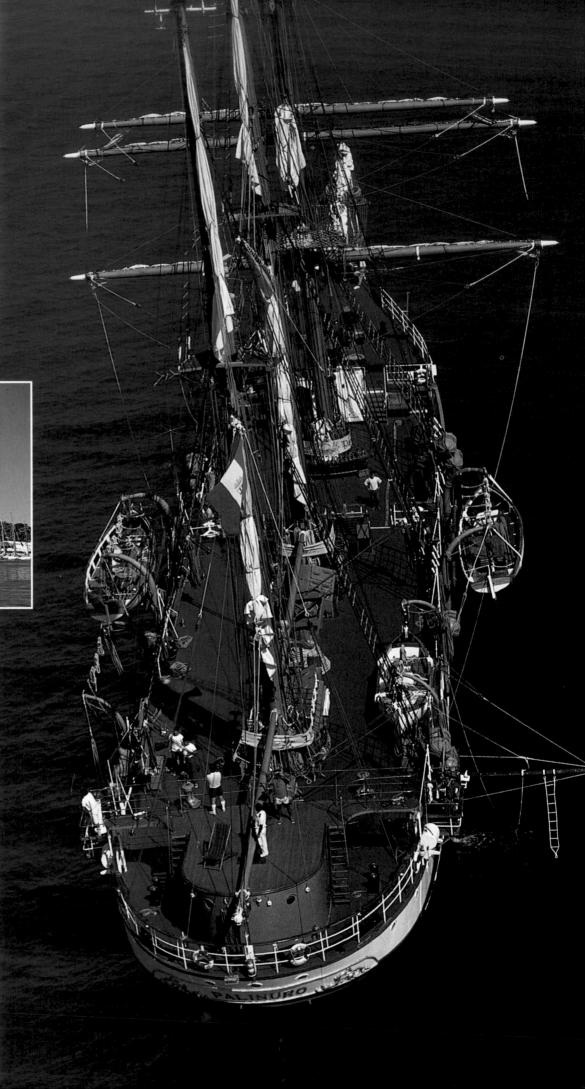

Pallada

Launched in 1989 by the shipyard at Gdansk, where Lech Walesa, the electrician who became president of the Polish People's Republic, once worked, the *Pallada* (ABOVE) was one of five vessels commissioned by the Soviet Union in the middle of the 1980s. The other sailing ships, all built to the plans that Zygmunt Choren had drawn up for the *Dar Mlodziezy*, were the *Mir* (launched in 1987), the *Khersones* and the *Druzhba* (launched with the *Pallada* in 1989), and the *Nadejda*, the youngest of the fleet, whose construction was completed in 1991. The *Pallada* and the *Nadejda* are based in Vladivostok, which is why they never appear in European waters. The *Pallada* stands apart from her sister ships in the color of her hull, which is painted black and decorated with deadlights. With a length of 109 meters, the ship carries a sail spread of three thousand square meters. It takes on 150 cadets with a regular crew of fifty. To facilitate maneuvering, Zygmunt Choren designed a detached spardeck (LEFT). The ship participated in the 1992 New York reunion to celebrate the five hundredth anniversary of Christopher Columbus's arrival in America. In March 1997, the Russian ship sailed in a race from Hong Kong to Osaka. The *Dar Mlodziezy* won the first leg, although it was only to take fifth place for the entire race. The *Pallada* beat the *Dar Mlodziezy* in the second leg. In effect, due to a different system of attaching its yardarms to its masts, the *Pallada* sails into the wind better than the *Dar Mlodziezy* does.

Pride of Baltimore II

During the American War of Independence, a new kind of sailing ship appeared off the coasts of Virgina: a speedy schooner that handled well (BELOW), sported a slender hull, a short freeboard, and masts that raked sharply to the rear (RIGHT, AND OPPOSITE), this new vessel was perhaps inspired by the French luggers that frequented those waters, or more likely by a kind of ship called a Bermuda sloop. The term "Baltimore-built" began to be applied to these fast schooners around the time of the War of 1812 between the English and the Americans, when these ships were at their zenith. Between 1835 and 1850, the schooners played an important role in the slave trade. It was during this time that the term "Baltimore Clipper" was first used. The *Pride of Baltimore II* is a reconstruction of this type of ship from the first half of the nineteenth century (FOLLOWING DOUBLE PAGE). In 1975, the city of Baltimore set out to reconstruct a replica of an 1812 Baltimore Clipper whose mission was to develop and promote the economic and cultural image of the city and of the state of Maryland. The future sailing ship was built by Thomas Gillmer in a shipyard that was opened to the public. Launched in 1977, the schooner successfully fulfilled its mission for more than a decade, during which time it voyaged 150,000 miles. Tragically, on July 14, 1986, a gust of wind with an estimated force of eighty knots overturned the boat and sank it with four of its

crew. But the construction of a new replica was quickly begun. The builders paid careful attention to the lessons its predecessor's fate, and added watertight bulkheads. Launched on April 30, 1988, the *Pride of Baltimore II* took up its ambassadorial mission. It sailed to Europe for the first time in 1990 and appeared there again in 1996.

Renard

Saint-Malo, the city of corsairs and privateers, was the domain of Robert Surcouf, the most infamous of the French pirates of the eighteenth century. After a very full and active life, largely spent hunting English vessels as far as the Indian Ocean, he retired to Saint-Malo and became one of France's wealthiest shipowners. In the twilight of his life he continued to

arm vessels that practiced piracy in the English Channel. In 1813 the last among these ships, a cutter named the *Renard*, sank the schooner *Alphea*, a British warship. When the citizens of Saint-Malo learned in 1987 that the neighboring port of Cancale had launched its new bisquine, they reacted immediately. What sailing ship could rival *La Cancalaise*, which had been the star of the reunion at Douarnenez in 1988? The Malouins decided to rebuild the *Renard*. Work began in May 1991 and was completed only three weeks before it sailed to take part in the gathering at Brest '92. Brightly painted and rigged as a topsail cutter, today it takes passengers for short voyages in the waters off Saint-Malo (RIGHT). The plan of the deck (ABOVE) and its twelve cannons evokes the cutters of the early nineteenth century.

Sagres II

The *Sagres II*, a Portuguese military training ship, is set apart from its sister ships by the immense red Portuguese crosses that are displayed on its square sails (BELOW). Based on the plans of the *Gorch Fock* (today the *Tovarishch*), the *Sagres II* was launched in 1937 for the German navy and was named the *Albert Leo Schlageter*. The ship was seized at the end of the Second World War by the Americans, who gave it to Brazil. Rechristened the *Guanabara*, it was refitted as a training ship. The Brazilians then sold it to the Portuguese in 1961. The Portuguese had been looking for a vessel to replace the aging first *Sagres* (launched in Germany in 1896), which had served the Portuguese navy since 1924. The first *Sagres* became a floating school and was renamed the *Santo André*. Its successor, the *Sagres II*, began its career with the cadets of the Portuguese navy in 1962. It has since called on ports throughout the world, sometimes taking on cadets from other nations. It circumnavigated the globe in 1978. In 1992, during a nine-month voyage, the *Sagres II* followed the route of Vasco da Gama, although it returned by way of the Suez Canal. The *Sagres II* participates

regularly in tall ship races; in the Columbus Race it followed the *Gorch Fock* on its departure from Cádiz (FOLLOWING DOUBLE PAGE). It also regularly participates in tall ship reunions (RIGHT). A statue of Henry the Navigator adorns its prow.

Sea Cloud

In the fleet of luxury yachts—the fantastic creations of the extremely wealthy—the *Sea Cloud* holds a special place (FOLLOWING DOUBLE PAGE). At the time of its construction, it was the largest sailing yacht ever built, measuring 109.5 meters in length. It was also the only yacht rigged as a four-masted bark. The *Sea Cloud* has survived an eventful life, which began at the end of the 1920s when Edward Francis Hutton decided to replace his *Hussar*, a seventy-two-meter, three-masted schooner, with a larger yacht. He commissioned the New York naval architects Gibbs

and Cox to draw up the plans. The construction of the yacht was awarded to Friedrich Krupp's Germania shipyard in Kiel, a yard that had considerable experience in the construction of both commercial ships and luxury yachts. The *Meteor*, the yacht of the emperor William II, had been built there, as well as the technologically advanced *Sedov*. The *Hussar*, launched on April 25, 1931, was a most opulent ship. The suite of Marjorie Merriweather Post, Hutton's wife, contained an Italian marble fireplace and gold-plated bathroom faucets in the shape of swans. Many of the yacht's exquisite appointments have been refurbished

in the course of its restorations (ABOVE, AND RIGHT). After its launch, the yacht sailed continuously until the couple's divorce in 1935. Edward Hutton offered the yacht to his former wife, who gave it the name *Sea Cloud*. Shortly afterward, she married Joseph E. Davies, an American politician. The *Sea Cloud* sailed to Leningrad in 1937, after Davies was appointed American ambassador to the Soviet Union. The American army requisitioned the yacht during the Second World War, removed its masts, and converted it into a meterological survey ship. The couple restored the yacht when it was returned to them

in 1944. Trujillo, the Dominican dictator, purchased it in 1957, and renamed it the *Angelita*. Trujillo's son sailed it to Los Angeles. After Trujillo was assassinated, the ship, remaining under the Dominican flag, was called the *Patria*. Several years later, an American consortium acquired it and gave it the name *Antama*, but it fell quickly into sad condition. A young American nevertheless succeeded in sailing it again, before it was finally abandoned in Panama. Purchased by a German buyer in 1979, it has since recovered its former glory and its name, *Sea Cloud*. It now offers deluxe cruises in the Antilles and the Mediterranean.

Sedov

Currently the world's largest sailing ship, the *Sedov* (RIGHT) is a four-masted bark. Like the *Sea Cloud*, it was built at the Germania shipyard in Kiel, but its stem-to-stern length surpasses by ten meters that of the luxury yacht. To its master helmsman, Constantinovich (BELOW), it is precious. The *Sedov* was built as a commercial ship. It was launched in 1921 for Karl Vinnen, who christened it with the name of his daughter, *Magdalene Vinnen*. Like many of its contemporaries, it made its first

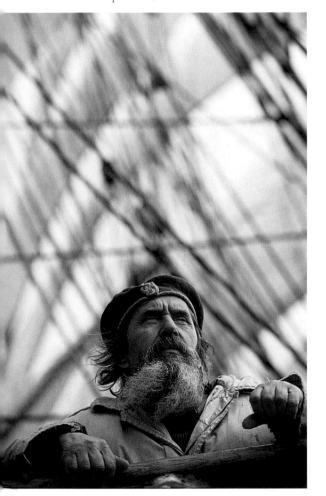

voyages to the coast of Chile where it took on cargoes of nitrates. It also voyaged in the Pacific Islands and to Australia to receive cargoes of cotton and wheat. It was sold in 1936 to the shipping company of Norddeutscher Lloyd, which renamed it the *Kommodore Johnsen* and refitted it for both the transport of Australian grain and the instruction of its future officers (FOLLOWING DOUBLE PAGE, LEFT TOP).

During World War II, it was converted into a training ship, but sailed only in summertime in the Baltic. The huge yards rigged to the fifty-eight-meter tall masts (LEFT, AND OPPOSITE, BOTTOM) cannot be braced by hand; they require a winding drum to secure them (ABOVE BOTTOM). Stowing the bowsprit jib remains a delicate task that can be dangerous in rough weather (ABOVE TOP). The British were awarded the ship as a war reparation in 1945, but gave it to the Russians, who had it towed in January 1946 to Liepaja on the west coast of Latvia, where its refurbishing was begun. It was then rechristened the *Sedov*, after Georgy Sedov, a Russian imperial navy officer who set off to conquer the North Pole in 1912 but died en route in 1914. The ship did not resume its

role as a training ship until 1952. In 1957, it took its cadets from Africa to the North Atlantic, and from the Antilles to the Mediterranean, on an international hydrographic mission. It made another exploratory voyage between 1962 and 1965, in the company of the *Kruzenshtern*. In 1965, the four-masted bark was assigned to the Soviet ministry of fisheries. The *Sedov* (PRECEDING DOUBLE PAGE) continued its mission as a training ship but was decommissioned at the end of 1971, the victim of escalating maintenance costs. Soviet authorities finally decided to overhaul and recondition the ship. It was placed in the charge of the shipyards on the island of Kronstadt, but did not leave in its modernized state until June 19, 1981. In 1986, it took part for the first time in a tall ship race. Two years later, it appeared in Douarnenez for a sailing reunion. In 1989, the *Sedov* accepted its first Western trainees, after more than

four thousand Soviet cadets had already been initiated on board. They learned to scrub the ship's decks, a chore that is still a part of a sailor's life (ABOVE). In 1992, the *Sedov* participated in the Columbus Race (RIGHT). Due to a lack of operating funds, the Russians decommissioned the ship in 1993, but substantial German funding made possible a thorough refitting in 1994. This was completed in a shipyard in former East Germany. Troubles have not entirely vanished, however. In June 1997, at the time of a port call in Cherbourg, the crew had not been paid for several months.

Shabab Oman

The *Shabab Oman*, whose name signifies "youth of Oman" (LEFT, AND ABOVE), was built in 1971 for a Scottish association. The Omanese navy purchased it in 1977 to preserve the sultanate of Oman's ancient mari-

time traditions. The country has no naval academy, and the thirty-one cadets, from seventeen to twenty-five years of age, who serve on board come from different corps of the Omanese army. The cadets assist eighteen crew members and five sailors. The ship's role is not limited to training; it also functions as its country's ambassador. In this role, the *Shabab Oman* has already made voyages to more than twenty countries. In 1986 it sailed to New York to celebrate the one hundredth anniversary of the Statue of Liberty, and in 1992 it took part in the five hundredth anniversary of Christopher Columbus's arrival in America. In January 1988, it participated in Sydney's festivities celebrating the bicentennial of Australia. In 1989 and 1994, the *Shabab Oman* took part in the tall ship reunions in Rouen.

Shenandoah

The three-masted schooner *Shenandoah*
(ABOVE BOTTOM, AND LEFT) was launched
in 1902 for Gibson Fahnestock, an
American financier. Between 1912 and
1952, the ship passed through the
hands of a variety of millionaire
owners before it was finally put to
work as a freighter in South America.
It was purchased several years later by a
French banker. Legal problems led to
the banker's imprisonment and the
seizure of the ship in 1962. It was then
abandoned in Cannes for nine years
before it was bought in 1971 and
restored by the Baron Marcel Biche
(ABOVE TOP), who used it as the head-
quarters of the French campaign for
the America's Cup. The baron's son
chartered the ship in the early 1980s.
After a thorough refurbishing, the
boat has been based in Monaco since
early 1997.

Simon Bolívar

Following the example of the *Esmeralda* in 1954 and the *Gloria* in 1967, other Latin American countries sought to acquire prestigious sailing ships to train their naval cadets and to represent their nations at great international meetings. Ecuador took delivery of the *Guayas* in 1976, and Venezuela received the *Simon Bolívar* the following year. The *Simon Bolívar* (FOLLOWING DOUBLE PAGE) is somewhat larger than its predecessors, measuring 82.3 meters from stem to stern, and carrying 1,850 square meters of sail. The ship immediately assumed its duties as a training vessel and as its country's seagoing ambassador. It is a spectacle at the international meets, with its cadets perched on its yardarms and its enormous national banner (LEFT). The cadets wear yellow, blue, or red T-shirts, which correspond to the colors of the Venezuelan flag and to their watch positions on board. On its first extended voyage, the *Simon Bolívar* sailed to Europe in 1980. It attended Philadelphia's tricentennial in 1983 and in 1984 took part in the first race of tall ships between Bermuda and Halifax, in Canada. It returned to Europe for Sail Amsterdam in 1985, and voyaged to New York the following year for the Statue of Liberty's anniversary. There, for the first time, it found itself in the company of its three sister ships launched from the same shipyard: the *Guayas*, the *Gloria*, and the *Cuauhtémoc*. Two years later, the *Simon Bolívar* crossed the ocean to help Australia celebrate its bicentennial. It did not take the shortest route to arrive there; instead, it sailed first to visit European ports. When it returned to its home port of Güira, near Caracas, it had completed a voyage around the world. At Sail Liberty and at the Liberty Armada, in 1989 and 1994 in Rouen, its festive crew charmed the citizens of the French port. The ship's superb reception salons make a lasting impression on the lucky few who are privileged to visit them. The *Simon Bolívar* also competed in the Columbus Race in 1992.

Sørlandet

The *Sørlandet* (BELOW, AND RIGHT) was built at the shipyard of Høivolds Mek, Versted A/S, in Kristiansand, in Norway, for the merchant marine academy of that city. It was financed by a Norwegian shipping line, AOT Skjelbred, on the condition that it not be equipped with an engine. It was launched in 1927. The North Sea was its preferred domain, although it did make long voyages beyond. In 1933, the *Sørlandet* sailed to Chicago where it represented Norway at the World's Fair. Afterward, it toured the Great Lakes. When war broke out in Europe in 1939, the ship was requisitioned by the Norwegian royal navy and was based at a naval dockyard in Horten, near Oslo. The Germans seized it in 1940 and moved it to Kirkenes, in the north of the country, where it was used as a prison ship. The *Sørlandet* sank in circumstances that have remained mysterious. The Germans raised it and brought it back to Kristiansand, where it was used as a barracks for their submariners. It was refurbished at the end of the war. The merchant marine academy at Kristiansand recommissioned it in 1947. In 1956, it took part in the first tall ship race, organized between

Torbay, England and Lisbon, Portugal. The *Sørlandet* had always remained purely a sailing vessel. It was only in 1960 that an engine was installed. It became a regular participant in international racing meets, even winning a leg of a race in 1966. The merchant marine academy that originally had commissioned it decided in 1973 to let it go. Jan Staubo, a Norwegian shipper, acquired it to prevent its sale abroad. In 1977,

Kristian Skjelbred-Knudsen, the grandson of the philanthropist who had financed its construction, purchased the ship and made a gift of it to the city of Kristiansand, which elected to recommission it as a civil sailing school. It went back to sea in 1981, reserved off season for the training of officers of the royal navy, and open to the public during the summer months. It is the first square-rigged three-master to accept civilians

on board for training in seamanship. In 1991, the foundation that manages it organized a training program in square-rigger sailing that was open to merchant marine sailors worldwide. The *Sørlandet* participated in Operation Sail in New York in 1986. The Norwegian three-master was present at Rouen in 1989 and 1994 (BELOW, AND RIGHT), and at Brest in 1992. It spent the winter of 1996 with trainees in the Antilles and returned there in 1998.

Star of India

A historic monument since 1966, the *Star of India* (LEFT, AND FOLLOWING DOUBLE PAGE) is preserved afloat in San Diego. It was one of the first sailing ships produced with a metal hull and is the oldest one today that is still in condition to sail (BELOW, LEFT AND RIGHT). Never equipped with an engine, the ship, launched in 1863, still ventures out to sea. Since 1976, the year that its most recent restoration was completed, it has sailed ten times. Nothing promised it so long a life; in fact, it has had a troubled history. In its first voyage, then under the name *Euterpe* (RIGHT), it collided with a Spanish vessel in the waters off Liverpool and the rigging of its mizzenmast was gravely damaged. During its second voyage, which lasted ten years, it lost its three masts and its captain in a hurricane. Since then, it has changed hands several times. A Cape Horner and a circum-navigator, it was removed from service in 1923 and was given to the San Diego Maritime Museum in 1957.

Statsraad Lehmkuhl

The *Statsraad Lehmkuhl* is today the world's largest three-masted bark (LEFT, AND BELOW). At ninety-eight meters in length, it was launched in Germany in 1914 under the name *Großherzog Friedrich August*. It was the third ship that a German association of training vessels accepted for the training of the imperial merchant

marine's cadets. The first vessel, the *Großherzogin Elisabeth*, was launched in 1901. Given to France after World War II, the ship was renamed the *Duchesse Anne*. The French navy gave the *Duchesse Anne* to the city of Dunkirk in 1981, which restored it and opened it to the public. The second ship, the *Prinzess Eitel Friedrich*, was launched in 1909. It served as a sailing trainer in Poland after the war and has been converted into a museum in Gdynia, Poland, under the name *Dar Pomorza*. The *Großherzog*

Friedrich August had made its first voyage with cadets when the First World War broke out. It spent the four following years at dock. In 1919 and 1920, it again set sail with German cadets, but Great Britain then received it as a war reparation. It was sold in 1923 to a shipper's association in Bergen. Given the name the *Statsraad Lehmkuhl*, it was again fitted out as a sail training school and was transferred to the Bergen sail training school foundation. Seized for wartime use in 1940, it sailed under the German flag, renamed the *Westwärts*, and was used as a warehouse. Returned to the Bergen Foundation at the end of the war, the ship resumed its training duties. It participated in several tall ship races before the Foundation was forced to give it up in 1966. A shipper, Hilmar Reksten, purchased it and financed its activities until 1972. Taken out of commission in 1975, it was given in 1978 to the Statsraad Lehmkuhl foundation, whose name the ship once again carries. The ship serves today as a sailing school, and takes on trainees in the summer (ABOVE TOP) who still sleep in hammocks (ABOVE BOTTOM). A regular participant in reunions and races, it came to the gatherings at Brest in 1992 and 1996 (RIGHT).

Swan fan Makkum

The *Swan fan Makkum* is the largest brig-schooner sailing in the world today (BELOW, AND RIGHT). It was built in 1993 at Gdansk in Poland. Its owner achieved his dream of having a sailing ship that would be eligible to compete in tall ship races. But the Dutch ship also voyages as a charter, especially in the Antilles during the winter months. The square sails of the mizzenmast furl themselves on a roller installed inside the yardarm, thereby freeing the crew from having to climb up into the rigging to set and haul them in. *Swan fan Makkum* first took part in a tall ship race in 1995. In 1996, she won the Penzanze-l'Aber Wrac'h Regatta, a race whose competitors included a number of the traditional vessels that gathered for Brest '96. A magnificent figure of a swan embellishes her prow.

Thendara

In 1936, Sir Arthur Young, a British parliamentarian with a reputation as a fine yachtsman, commissioned the naval architect Alfred Mylne to design a sailing yacht. A ketch, carrying a fore-and-aft rigging, it was launched in 1937. *Thendara* (LEFT) shone in the first regattas in which it participated. Young also cruised for pleasure around the Anglo-Normand islands, to the north of Brittany, and in the Bay of Biscay. During the Second World War, the royal navy requisitioned *Thendara*. When the yacht was returned after the war, with compensation to repair the damage that the craft had suffered, Young entrusted *Thendara* to a Scottish shipyard, charging it to replace the yacht's stem-post and a section of its broadsides. Sir Arthur continued to compete in regattas and to cruise on his yacht until he died aboard in 1950. The ketch was sold and sailed the Greek islands. Between 1986 and 1988, its new Australian owner made major

repairs to the yacht at La Spezia shipyard, in Italy. The yacht was sold once again several months later to Mike Horsley, a specialist in the sale and management of luxury yachts, who placed the restoration of the yacht in the hands of a shipyard at Southampton. Executed with respect for Alfred Mylne's design, the restoration included several necessary compromises. The installation of the most modern equipment—air conditioning, a desalinization unit, and navigation gear—remained perfectly discrete. The interior fittings were designed with care for historic authenticity. The rigging was refurbished to be identical with the original; one notable accomplishment is the successful restoration of the yacht's gaff sails. *Thendara* today cruises the waters of Europe and joins in prestigious regattas such as Saint-Tropez's La Nioulargue (ABOVE) or the Atlantic Challenge Cup '97, a transatlantic race organized with the express aim of breaking the time record held since 1905 by the schooner *Atlantic*.

Tovarishch

In 1933, the Hamburg shipyard of Blohm & Voß launched a three-masted bark, the *Gorch Fock*, to replace the *Niobe*. The *Niobe* had been assigned to train German navy cadets, but had sunk several months earlier, taking sixty-nine sailors with it. Scuttled in 1945, the *Gorch Fock* was given to the Soviets, who repaired the ship. Renamed the *Tovarishch* in 1950, it was based at Kherson on the Black Sea. Recommissioned as a sailing school, it at times made long voyages to faraway destinations such as India, the Cape of Good Hope, and the United States. It took part in a tall ship racing event for the first time in 1974. Her exploitation, however, posed more and more problems to the Soviet authorities. Following in the steps of the *Sedov* and the *Kruzenshtern*, in 1991 the *Tovarishch* was opened to Westerners (OPPOSITE). The Soviets understood the importance of keeping in service ships that, however old, were crowned with aesthetic and historic laurels. In this regard, the *Tovarishch* stood apart from the less opulent *Mir* and her sister ships. The *Tovarishch* passed into Ukrainian hands in 1992. At the start of the Columbus Race in Cádiz that summer, the yardarm of her main royal split in half (RIGHT). The crew took on the task of repairing it at sea, in order to prepare it for the tall ship reunion in New York. In 1994, it was forbidden to sail, and now is confined to its mooring in Britain, where it awaits generous benefactors who will finance its restoration and permit it once again to set out to sea.

Velsheda

Built for W. F. Stephenson at the Camper & Nicholsons shipyard in Gosport, England, *Velsheda*, whose name was formed from the first syllables of the first names of the owner's three daughters—Velma, Sheila, and Daphne—was launched in 1933. It is a J Class yacht of *grande classe*, one of the giants that were produced in the 1930s in spite of the economic crises of that time. This class of yacht was established by the New York Yacht Club to define which sailing yachts were eligible to participate in the America's Cup. *Velsheda*, spreading 730 square meters of sail for a length of 23.5 meters, won many regattas during the four seasons it participated, but it never competed for the America's Cup. Then, for many years, the ship was idle. Finally, in the 1980s, the yacht was brought up out of the mud of the Hamble River in Great Britain, where it had rested in disrepair. Restored, it was universally admired at the gathering in 1988 in Douarnenez. The height of its mast rose above that of the *Belem*! Since then *Velsheda* has taken part in numerous classic yacht regattas (LEFT, AND ABOVE). An important refurbishing in 1997 restored it to pristine condition.

Zawisza Czarny II

In 1934, the Polish union of Sea Scouts purchased a wooden Swedish schooner that had been launched in 1901 under the name *Petrea*. They renamed it the *Zawisza Czarny*. In 1965 the Sea Scouts decided to acquire a new vessel. The group bought a fishing boat that had been built in 1952 by the Cietrzew shipyard at Gdansk, and converted it into a three-masted staysail schooner. This vessel's crew has dedicated itself to preserving maritime folklore—especially the rich legacy of music and dance—associated with life at sea. Their mission has made the *Zawisza Czarny II* one of the most musical of ships at reunions. Navigating for the most part in the Baltic Sea, the *Zawisza Czarny II* (RIGHT) has nevertheless competed in numerous tall ship races that have taken her far from her home waters. In 1984, it won its category of the race from Saint-Malo to Bermuda. In the next stage of the same race, Bermuda to Halifax, her crew saved eight survivors of the sinking of the British ship the *Marques*, and returned them safely to Bermuda. The schooner again crossed the Atlantic in 1992, to participate in the Columbus Race. Before returning to Europe, it cruised along the coast of Labrador. The ship also took part in the Mediterranean race in 1996, where it was awarded a prize for having the youngest crew.

Glossary

ASTROLABE
A metal instrument conceived by the Greeks around 200 B.C., the astrolabe was used for solving problems in astronomy and navigation, especially for measuring the height of a heavenly body from the horizon in order to calculate latitude. It was impractical because of its weight, imprecision, and the difficulty of holding it steadily on moving vessels.

ATHWARTSHIPS
At right angles to the centerline of a boat.

BACKSTAY
Any of various ropes or metal cables of the standing rigging which lead aft to the sides and stern of a vessel to support the upper masts (topmast, royal mast, and skysail mast) against forward pull.

BARK
A three-masted vessel with a square-rigged foremast and mainmast and a fore-and-aft-rigged mizzenmast. Four-masted ships that are fore-and-aft-rigged on the spanker mast are sometimes called four-masted barks.

BARKENTINE
A three-masted vessel with a square-rigged foremast and two fore-and-aft-rigged aftermasts.

BATTERY
Originally a deck on which two rows of canon (starboard and port) were installed, today it is often the deck where crews and cadets in training are quartered on the great sailing ships.

BEAM
A transverse structural member of a vessel's framework fixed to its ribs to support its deck. The maximum beam (width) of a vessel is the length of its longest transverse beam.

BISQUINE (*See* FISHING SMACK)

BITT
A heavy, firmly mounted fixture of wood or metal for securing lines.

BLOCK
A wood or metal fixture which encloses one or more freely rotating, grooved pulleys (sheaves), through which running rigging (cables, chains, or ropes) passes to form a hoisting or hauling tackle.

BOLLARD
A heavy post set into a wharf or pier to which the lines of a ship may be made fast.

BOOM
A horizontal spar for extending the feet of sails (especially fore-and-aft sails), or for shifting cargo, extending mooring lines, etc.

BOWSPRIT
An oblique spar extending from a vessel's bow to which the foremast stays and the tacks of various jibs are stretched.

BRIG
A two-masted square-rigged sailing vessel.

BRIGANTINE
Vessel: A two-masted vessel, square-rigged on the foremast with a fore-and-aft mainsail and square upper sails.
Sail: A triangular spanker sail rigged on the mizzenmast on sailing vessels with three or more masts.

BROADSIDE CONSTRUCTION
A technique in which the sides of a ship are built first and then attached to a frame. Used in the ancient Mediterranean and later in the construction of the clinker-built boats of Northern Europe.

BROADSIDES
The sides of a vessel, the strakes of wood planking or the sheet metal attached to its framework, which together form its hull from the bow to the quarter above the waterline.

CADET
A student on a civil or military training vessel.

CAPSTAN
A wood or metal windlass mounted to the deck and around which is wound heavy rope. Turned by hand (sometimes electrically), it is used in such operations as taking in a hawser or hoisting sail.

CARAVEL

A rapid sailing vessel of the fifteenth and sixteenth centuries, lateen-rigged on two or three masts, and generally of Spanish or Portugese origin, it incorporated late medieval technical advances such as framework construction and stern rudders.

CARRACK/CARAQUE

A merchant ship common especially in the Mediterranean from the late Middle Ages until the end of the sixteenth century, it usually carried three or four masts and had a forecastle which projected over the stem.

CASTLE

The forecastle and the poop deck of ships from the sixteenth to eighteenth centuries. The elevation of these superstructures diminished over time, disappearing almost entirely by 1800.

CLEW

The lower aft corner of a sail.

CLINKER CONSTRUCTION

A method of hull construction in which the shell is formed of clinker planking where each strake overlaps the one below.

CLIPPER

A fast sailing ship developed in the United States in the 1840s, it had a sleek hull, tall raked masts, an expansive spread of sail, and an extended bow.

COMPASS

A navigation instrument which shows the heading of the ship by means of a freely rotating magnetized needle oriented to magnetic north.

COMPASS CARD (*dial, mariner's card*)

A magnetized, freely rotating circular card floating suspended from a pivot within the bowl of a compass. Its face is graduated around its rim in a star-shaped diagram representing the thirty-six degrees (clockwise from north) of the wind.

CROSS-JACK

A large square sail rigged below the mizzen-topmast on schooners and the maintopmast of a ketch.

CROSS-STAFF (*forestaff, Jacob's staff*)

A simple instrument of wood, consisting of a calibrated staff with a shorter, slide-adjusted perpendicular staff, which served to determine by direct observation the angle of elevation of a star measured from the horizon and thereby to calculate latitude, usually by determining the position of the polar star.

CROSSTREE

Placed athwart a lower masthead's trestletrees, one of a pair of wood or metal bars from which are spread shrouds leading to the mast above and/or serving to support a platform or top.

CUTWATER

The knee of a ship's head at the forward edge of a vessel's bow, it slices through the water as the vessel advances. It can also serve as a support for a figurehead at the prow and to support the extension of a bowsprit.

DECK HOUSE

An enclosed structure rising above the deck but surrounded on all sides by exposed deck area, not reaching across its entire width.

FAIRLEAD

A fixture, usually of metal with rounded edges, installed on the deck to guide a vessel's running rigging and mooring lines and to protect them from chafing.

FISHING SMACK

Any of various small, fully decked, fore-and-aft-rigged vessels used for trawling or coastal trading, often with a well for keeping fish alive. Called a BISQUINE, rigged as a lugger, and formerly in use in the ports around the Bay of Mont-Saint-Michel in France—most notably Granville and Cancale—for bottom fishing, trawling, and oyster dragging.

FOOT

The bottom edge of a sail.

FOREMAST

The mast nearest the bow in all vessels having two or more masts.

FORESAIL

The principal (lowermost) sail carried on the foremast of schooners and sailing ships with three or more masts. It also refers to the staysail, or jib set, immediately forward of the mainmast of a cutter, ketch, sloop, or yawl.

FORE-AND-AFT SAIL

Any sail (jibs, jib-headed sails, gaff sails, lugsails, lateen sails, and staysails) that is not set on a yard, and is normally set in a fore-and-aft direction amidships.

Gorch Fock

Forecastle

A superstructure at or immediately after the bow of a ship, used as a shelter for stores, machinery, etc., or as quarters for crew.

Foretopmast staysail

A sail whose clew line is secured to the forecastle, as opposed to a jib whose clew line is attached to the bowsprit.

Frame construction

A shipbuilding technique in which the framework is built before the sides.

Freeboard

The surface of the hull between the waterline and the level of the main deck.

Frigate

A ship-rigged naval vessel intermediate in size between a corvette and a ship of the line, the frigate came into use around 1750, armed with a full battery on the gun deck and often a light battery on the spar deck. The largest of these ships, double-banked frigates or double bankers, carried up to fifty guns in batteries on two decks with a flush upper deck. Even larger and more powerful steam frigates dominated the world's navies from the 1850s until about 1870.

Gaff

An oblique spar rising aft from a mast to support the head of a quadrilateral fore-and-aft (gaff) sail.

Galleon

A two-to-five-hundred-ton three-masted naval and commercial ship of the sixteenth and seventeenth centuries, often with three or four decks, principally engaged in the service of Spain for the transport of riches originating in its American colonies.

Galley

A large, low, shallow-draft vessel, relatively inexpensive to build, usually with one deck, propelled by both oars and sails. Used primarily in the Mediterranean for war and trade from antiquity until the end of the Middle Ages, it last played a major role in 1571 at the great naval battle of Lepanto. The typical Mediterranean war galley was from thirty-five to seventy meters in length, often having as many as thirty oars on each side with many rowers to each oar. It had two or three masts rigged with lateen sails, carried guns at prow and stern, and a crew often exceeding one thousand men.

Handspike

A bar used as a lever which is inserted in a capstan-bar hole and serves to turn it.

Hawser

A heavy rope used to moor or tow vessels.

Helm

The wheel or tiller controlling the rudder of a vessel.

Hull

The hollow, lowermost portion of a vessel, floating immersed (partially) in the water and supporting the rest of the vessel.

Jib

A triangular staysail, whose clew line is attached to the bowsprit or to the jib boom, set forward of a forestaysail or a foretopmast staysail—flying jib, inner jib, outer jib.

Keel

A ship's backbone and central structural member, extending at the base of the hull from the stem to the sternpost, to which the framework or ribs are attached.

Ketch

A two-masted fore-and-aft-rigged sailing vessel which carries its mainmast forward and its mizzenmast or jiggermast stepped forward of the rudderpost to the rear. It is similar to a yawl, but its mizzenmast is stepped farther forward and it has a larger mizzen.

Lighter (*sailing barge, scow*)

A freight vessel, generally an unpowered, flat-bottomed rectangular barge, designed for the transport of heavy merchandise—casks of wine, sand, etc.—and whose different types are designed for short distance river or coastal navigation.

Lightship

A vessel fitted with a light or lights and anchored in a specific location where it serves as a beacon to guide mariners.

Lugger

A vessel carrying one or more lugsails with as many as three masts with or without jibs and/or topsails.

Mainmast

The second mast from forward in any vessel with two or more masts. In a ketch or yawl the

mainmast is stepped forward of the second mast; in single-masted vessels, such as sloops or cutters, the single mast is the mainmast. On a ketch the mainmast is placed in front, on a schooner to the rear; on a three-masted vessel, it is in the middle. Ships with four or more masts can have two or more mainmasts.

MAST

A spar of wood or metal set on the keel and rising through the decks above the hull and upper portions of a vessel to hold sails, spars, rigging, etc., at some point on the fore-and-aft line, as a foremast, a mainmast, or a mizzenmast. The mast is usually set up in approximate perpendicularity to the keel, but in some vessels, especially those using lateen sails, it may have considerable slant, or rake, forward or aft. Masts of one length are called pole masts. Masts made up of several pieces bound together are called made or built-up masts. In larger sailing vessels masts are usually made in several lengths, one rising above the other, and the upper lengths so arranged as to be lowered when needed. From the deck these lengths are named lower mast, topmast, topgallant mast, and royal mast.

MIZZEN

The rearmost mast on a yawl or ketch, or on sailing ships which carry two or more masts. Also, a sail set on that mast.

NEF

A merchant vessel active in the Mediterranean during the Middle Ages. Rounded in form, twenty-five to thirty-five meters in length, it usually carried only one mast rigged with a lateen sail. Crusaders sailed nefs to the Holy Land.

OCTANT

A instrument with an arc of 24 degrees used by navigators to measure angles of up to 90 degrees, invented by the Englishman Hadley in 1730 to determine the position of a star with more precision than was possible with the cross-staff. With the octant, the star was no longer directly observed but was reflected in a mirror. The position of a star could be read on a graduated scale when its reflected image was aligned with the horizon. The sextant gradually replaced the octant in the second half of the eighteenth century.

POOP

The part of the hull and a vessel's superstructure that extends behind the rearmost extension of the keel.

POOP DECK

A weather deck on top of a poop.

PORTHOLE (*gunport, embrasure*)

An opening in the hull of a ship which permitted the projection of canon. When a ship was not engaged in combat, these ports were closed by means of panels which opened out toward the exterior. Also, any of various (usually glass-covered) openings in the side of a ship or its superstructures for light, ventilation, etc.

PORT

Facing forward, to the left side of a vessel.

PROW

The part of the hull that extends forward of the keel.

QUARTERDECK

The part of the weather deck that runs aft from amidships or the mainmast to the stern of a vessel's poop.

RANK

The classification of warships established in the seventeenth century. The rank of a ship was determined by the number of artillery pieces installed on its decks, and sometimes also by the caliber of the canon and the size of the crews which served on them.

REEF (*reef line or band*)

A horizontal section of a sail which can be pulled in independently of the rest of the sail to reduce the sail surface in response to wind and weather conditions.

TO RIG (*a mast, vessel, etc.*)

The operations of setting up the masts, yardarms, fixed and running rigging, spars, sails, pulleys, blocks, and deck fittings of a vessel. Rigging a sail refers to setting, orienting, hoisting, or furling a sail. *To rig down*: to put a vessel's rigging in an inactive state, stowing all sails, lines, tackles, and other removable parts. *To rig up*: to put a vessel's rigging in an active state.

RIGGING

The type of sail which a boat carries but also the ensemble of its masts, spars, yardarms and lines, sails—all that is used in the propulsion, securing, fastening, and mooring of the ship. The standing rigging is the ensemble of lines— either rope or metal—that hold the masts and spars in position. The running rigging is the ensemble of lines which serve in maneuvering the spars and in setting, hoisting, furling, and shifting sails.

SCHOONER
A fore-and-aft-rigged vessel, capable of sailing close to the wind, a schooner generally has two masts, with the smaller sail set on the foremast and the mainmast stepped nearly amidships. Longer fore-and-aft-rigged ships with up to seven masts are referred to as three-masted, four-masted schooners, etc.

SEXTANT
An instrument of navigation derived from the octant, the sextant came into use during the second half of the eighteenth century. It was used to measure angular distances, especially the altitudes of the sun, moon, and stars at sea to determine latitude and longitude.

SHEER
The camber of a vessel's decks. The sheer is pronounced when the edges of the deck are much higher than the level of the deck in the middle of the ship. Also, the fore-and-aft upward curve of the hull of a vessel at the main deck or bulwarks.

SHIP OF THE LINE
A large warship, superior to a frigate, endowed with powerful artillery, usually a seventy-four-gun three-decker but often carrying an even greater weight of artillery. Opposing naval forces would position their first-ranked ships in two parallel lines and try to destroy each other with artillery fire.

SHEAVE
A grooved wheel or pulley set in a block for hoisting or hauling rope or cable.

SHROUD
Standing rigging that supports a mast athwartships, any of a number of taut ropes or metal cables converging from both sides of a vessel on the head of a lower or upper mast.

SLOOP
A fore-and-aft-rigged vessel with one mast and a single headsail jib.

SPANKER
A fore-and-aft sail set upon the mizzenmast of a three-masted vessel, and the jiggermast of a four-masted vessel. There is no spanker in a one- or two-masted vessel of any rig. Also called a "driver" in archaic usage.

SPAR
A general term for masts, yards, booms, gaffs, etc.

SPAR DECK
The upper deck from the prow to the poop of a vessel with neither forecastle nor poop deck. A spar deck may be fitted with deck houses.

SPRITSAIL
A square sail that was rigged under the bowsprit of ships in the seventeenth and eighteenth centuries.

STARBOARD
Facing forward, to the right side of a vessel.

STAY
A rope or metal cable on which run the spreading rings of a staysail. A metal cable or strong rope which holds a mast upright.

STEM
An upright member at the bow of a vessel into which the side plates or timbers are jointed.

STEMPOST
A vertical wooden beam which extends the keel to the bow of a ship.

STERN GALLERY
An open platform at the stern of a ship, below the level of the quarter-deck.

STERNPOST
An upright member rising from the after end of the keel.

STORESHIP
A large merchant vessel of Dutch origin with a rounded stern, low-slung fore- and afterdecks, and reduced tophamper. These seaworthy ships could be fitted with cannon when necessary, but often voyaged unarmed in order to carry more freight.

STUDDING-SAIL
A light supplementary square sail occasionally rigged on a boom projecting from the end of a yardarm to increase the sail surface.

SUPERSTRUCTURE
A ship's upper works, topsides, poop and forecastle—any structure built above the main deck of a ship as a continuation of its sides.

TACK
The lower forward corner of a triangular sail.

TACKING LINE
Originally, the rope which served to open a square sail to windward. By extension the expressions "port tack" and "starboard tack" are used to indicate the side from which the wind is coming.

TONNAGE
International unit of the capacity of ships. First a unit of weight approximately corresponding to one ton (deadweight tons), it became a unit of volume in the eighteenth century. Today a ton is the equivalent of 2.83 cubic meters of volume (gross tons).

TOP
The platform placed at the top of the lower mast, upon which rests the upper mast, called the topmast.

TOPHAMPER
The surface of the rigging, superstructure, and hull of a ship which is exposed to the force of wind. The tophamper, in relation to its significance, causes a leeway drift.

TOPMAN
Originally referring to a sailor who worked on the topyard and above, it now refers to any sailor assigned to the maneuvering of a tall ship.

TOPMAST
The next mast above a lower mast, usually formed of a separate spar from the lower mast and used to support the yards or rigging of a topsail or topsails. This mast is maintained in position by stays running in front of it, by shrouds which are attached to the top platform, and by back stays which are fastened athwartships to the rear to the bulwarks or the hull.

TOPSAIL
A square sail placed immediately above the mainsail on a square-rigged ship. Tall ships generally carry two topsails on each mast: a fixed lower topsail and an upper topsail whose yardarm is hoisted up along the length of the mast. Upper and lower topsails are further distinguished by the masts on which they are rigged: fore upper and lower topsails, mizzen upper and lower topsails, and main upper and lower topsails.

TRUCK (of a mast)
A circular or square piece of wood or metal fixed on the head of a mast (or at the top of the topmast section of a mast when a mast is divided into two or more sections), usually containing small holes for signal halyards.

WARPING CHOCK
Any of various heavy metal fittings on a deck or wharf that serve as fairleads for cables or chains.

WINCH
A small capstan used by hand on yachts. A windlass turned by a crank for hoisting or hauling.

YARD
A long spar, supported more or less at its center, to which the head of a square sail, lateen sail, or lugsail is bent.

YARDARM
A horizontal spar on which is fastened a square sail. The yardarm takes the name of the sail which it supports, e.g., the main yardarm for the mainsail and the lower foretopsail yardarm for the lower foretopsail.

YAWL
A two-masted fore-and-aft-rigged sailing vessel having a large mainmast and a smaller jiggermast or mizzenmast stepped abaft the sternpost.

Organizations

Such organizations as the nineteen national sail training associations affiliated through the International Sail Training Association (ISTA), and museums at historic ports throughout the world—including Bristol and Portsmouth in Great Britain, and Mystic Seaport in the United States—are all participants in the Renaissance of Sail.

The American Sail Training Association and the International Yacht Restoration School are examples of organizations that are working to preserve the world's maritime heritage and to share its rich history with everyone.

AMERICAN SAIL TRAINING ASSOCIATION
P.O. Box 1459
Newport, R.I. 02840
Phone (401) 846-1775; Fax (401) 849-5400
http://tallships.sailtraining.org

The American Sail Training Association (ASTA) is the oldest organization in the Americas devoted to furthering the goals and practice of sail training, and represents some 150 tall ships hailing from ports in North and South America.

ASTA annually organizes Tall Ships Events, Conferences and Seminars, and a variety of publications. Contact ASTA for more information on how you can set sail.

Hundreds of thousands of people of all ages and backgrounds set sail each year aboard a wide range of unique vessels to relive maritime history, study the marine arts and sciences firsthand, or to embark on the adventure of a lifetime. Sail training is a powerful tool in building leadership qualities, nurturing teamwork skills, and instilling a deep reverence for nature. ASTA provides information, support, and promotion for sail training and education under sail in the Americas.

ASTA was the first of a current roster of nineteen national sail training associations affiliated through the International Sail Training Association (ISTA)—similar to national and international coordinating bodies in other sports. ASTA's mission is to "encourage character building through sail training, promote sail training to the American public, and support education under sail . . . " ASTA represents virtually all of the ships engaged in sail training in the United States and has a grassroots membership of individual supporters from throughout the country—even from those states without a coast.

Different from learning to sail, sail training enables learning from sailing. ASTA's member vessels are all engaged in education—from the marine arts and sciences to living history; corporate team building, leadership development, marine ecology—the possibilities are as endless as the horizon at the sea's edge. Long utilized by the navies of the world to develop strong leadership skills in young officers, sail training is now accessible to virtually anyone. Each year, more and more ships come on-line as various schools, muni-cipalities, museums, and other non-profit organizations incorporate the powerful ability of the sea to teach in their curricula.

INTERNATIONAL YACHT
RESTORATION SCHOOL
449 Thames Street
Newport, R.I. 02840
(401) 848-5777

The International Yacht Restoration School (IYRS, pronounced "iris") welcomes students and visitors from around the world. Its 2 1/2-acre waterfront site includes a National Historic Register Steam Mill Building, the IYRS Restoration Hall, the IYRS Gallery, and a beautiful wharf with numerous yachts on display.

A nonprofit organization, IRYS offers a range of programs for adults and students above the age of fourteen. Teaching the skills, history, and sciences involved in the construction, restoration, and maintenance of yachts, IYRS provides job training for the international boating industry and teaches teamwork, self-respect, and pride in good workmanship.

IYRS has certainly worked miracles in its splendid restorations of two of the three surviving J Class yachts: *Endeavour*, a 130-foot sloop launched in 1934 and renowned as the most beautiful J ever built, and *Shamrock V,* built in 1930 for Sir Thomas Lipton's fifth and last America's Cup challenge, the first J Class sloop ever built and the only remaining wooden J.

In the coming years the centerpiece project for IYRS will be the restoration of the last remaining great American yacht—*Coronet.* Coronet is 167 feet overall, 133 feet on deck, with a twenty-seven-foot beam, a twelve-foot draft, and 8,500 square feet of working sail area. She was built at the Poillon yard in Brooklyn for New York Yacht Club member Rufus T. Bush.

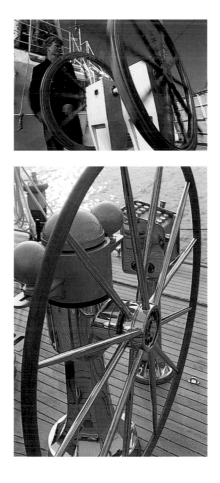

Bibliography

Abranson, Erik C. and Beken of Cowes. *Sailing Ships of the World.* Thomas Reed Publications, Ltd., 1992.

Anderson, R. C. *The Rigging of Ships in the Days of the Spritsail Topmast, 1600–1720.* (Illus.). Reprint ed. Dover,

Averitt, Max W., illus. *Boatwatch: Master Guide to Sailboats of the World.* (Illus.). Boatwatch, 1992.

Beken, Frank W. and Beken, Keith. *The Beauty of Sail, with One Hundred Full Page Photos of Yachts.* Gordon Press, 1972.

Biddlecombe, George. *Art of Rigging.* Dover, 1990.

Bishop, Paul. *Tall Ships and the Cutty Sark Races.* Aidan Ellis, 1994.

Blackburn, Graham. *The Illustrated Encyclopedia of Ships, Boats and Vessels.* (Illus.). Overlook Press, 1982.

Bobrow, Jill R. *Classic Yacht Interiors: A Reissue.* 5th ed. (Illus.). Reprint ed. Concepts Publishing, 1993.

Bobrow, Jill R. *The World's Most Extraordinary Yachts.* 4th ed. (Illus.). Reprint ed. Concepts Publishing, 1992.

Bosscher, Philip, ed. *The Heyday of Sail: The Merchant Sailing Ship, 1650–1830.* (Conway's History of the Ship Series). Naval Institute Press, 1996.

Bowen, F. C. *Wooden Walls in Action: The History of Ships from 1340 to 1866.* Gordon Press, 1977.

Braynard, Frank O. *The Tall Ships of Today in Photographs.* Dover, 1993.

Brookesmith, Frank. *I Remember the Tall Ships.* (Illus.). Sheridan, 1991.

Carrick, Robert W. *John G. Alden & His Yacht Designs.* International Marine, 1995.

Cipolla, Carlo M. *Guns, Sails, and Empires: Technological Innovations, and the Early Phases of European Expansion, 1400–1700.* 1965.

Chapelle, Howard I. *American Small Sailing Craft.* (Illus.). Norton, 1951.

Chapelle, Howard I. *The Baltimore Clipper: Its Origin and Development.* Marine Research Society, 1930.

Chapelle, Howard I. *Boatbuilding: A Complete Handbook of Wooden Boat Construction.* Norton, 1994.

Chapelle, Howard I. *Yacht Designing & Planning.* McGraw-Hill, 1996.

Chapman, Roger. *In the Eye of the Wind.* Hamish Hamilton, 1982.

Christensen, Arne E., ed. *The Earliest Ships: The Evolution of Boats into Ships.* (Conway's History of the Ship Series). (Illus.). Naval Institute Press, 1996.

Cooke, Edward W. *Sailing Vessels in Authentic Early Nineteenth-Century Illustration.* (Illus.). Dover, 1989.

Crothers, William L. *The American-Built Clipper Ship: Characteristics, Construction, & Details.* (Illus.). McGraw-Hill, 1996.

Culver, Henry B. *The Book of Old Ships: From Egyptian Galleys to Clipper Ships.* (Pictorial Archive Series). (Illus.). Unabridged ed. Dover, 1992.

Dana, Richard. *Two Years Before the Mast.* Various editions.

Davis, Charles G. *American Sailing Ships.* (Antique Series: Transportation). Dover, 1984.

Deane, Anthony N. *Nelson's Favorite: HMS Agamemnon 1789–1809.* (Illus.). Naval Institute Press, 1996.

Dear, Ian and Kemp, Peter K., eds. *An A-Z of Sailing Terms.* Abr. ed. (Illus.). Oxford University Press, 1992.

Editors. *Sail Last Century: The Merchant Sailing Ship, 1830–1930.* Conway Maritime Press, Ltd., 1993.

Fairburn, William A. *Merchant Sail,* vol. 1, *Early Days of Exploration and the Influence of Shipbuilding in the Development of the U.S.* Reprint ed. Higginson Book Company, 1992.

Fairburn, William A. *Merchant Sail,* vol. 3, *U.S. Merchant Sail-Types; Models & Rigs; Clippers & Square-Riggers of the Post-Clipper Period.* Reprint ed. Higginson Book Company, 1992.

Fairburn, William A. *Merchant Sail,* vol. 5, *U.S. Woodshipbuilders & Shipbuilding Centers Through the Nineteenth Century, Including Packets, Clippers & Down Easters.* Ritchie, Ethel M., ed. Reprint ed. Higginson Book Company, 1992.

Friel, Ian. *The Good Ship: Ships, Shipbuilding, & Technology in England, 1200–1520.* (Illus.). Johns Hopkins, 1995.

Gardiner, Robert. *The Heavy Frigate: Eighteen-Pounder Frigates, 1778–1800.* (Conway's Ship Type Series). (Illus.). Naval Institute Press, 1995.

Gibbs, Jim. *Pacific Square-Riggers.* (Illus.). Schiffer, 1987.

Gibbs, Jim. *Windjammers of the Pacific Rim.* Schiffer, 1987.

Giggal, Kenneth. *Classic Sailing Ships.* (Illus.). Norton, 1988.

Gillmer, Thomas. *Pride of Baltimore: The Story of the Baltimore Clippers.* International Marine, 1992.

Goldenberg, Joseph A. *Shipbuilding in Colonial America.* University Press of Virginia, 1976.

Goodman, David. *Spanish Naval Power, 1589–1665: Reconstruction & Defeat.* (Cambridge Studies in Early Modern History). (Illus.). Cambridge University Press, 1997.

Greenhill, Basil and Starkey, David J., eds. *The Evolution of the Sailing Ship, 1250–1589: Keynote Studies from* The Mariner's Mirror. (Illus.). Naval Institute Press, 1996.

Greenhill, Basil and Hackman, John. *The Grain Races: The Baltic Background.* Conway Maritime Press, Ltd., 1986.

Greenhill, Basil and Hackman, John. *Herzogin Cecilie: The Life and Times of a Four-masted Barque.* Conway Maritime Press, Ltd., 1991.

Grobecker, Bo and Neumann, Peter. *Sea Cloud: A Living Legend.* Collector's Books, Ltd., 1991.

Harding, Richard. *The Evolution of the Sailing Navy, 1509–1815.* (British History in Perspective Series). St. Martin, 1995.

Harrington, Melissa. *The New York Yacht Club: 1844–1994.* Robbins, Celia D., ed. (Illus.). Greenwich Publishing Group, 1994.

Hattendorf, John B. *Maritime History,* vol. I, *The Eighteenth Century and the Classic Age of Sail.* (Open Forum Series). (Illus.). Krieger, 1997.

Hays, Daniel and Hays, David. *My Old Man and the Sea: A Father and Son Sail Around Cape Horn.* Algonquin Books, 1995.

Henderson, Richard. *Philip L. Rhodes & His Yacht Designs.* (Illus.). International Marine, 1993.

Herreshoff, L. Francis. *Captain Nat Herreshoff: The Wizard of Bristol.* McGraw-Hill, 1996.

Hume, C. W. and Armstrong, M. C. *Cuttysark & Thermopylæ.* State Mutual, 1987.

Jackson, Gordon and Williams, David M., eds. *Shipping, Technology & Imperialism: Papers Presented to the Third British-Dutch Maritime History Conference.* (Illus.). Scholar Press, 1996.

Jones, Tristan. *The Incredible Voyage: A Personal Odyssey.* (Illus.). Sheridan, 1996.

Kemp, Peter K., ed. *The Oxford Companion to Ships and the Sea.* (Illus.). Oxford University Press, 1994.

Kinney, Francis. *The Best of the Best: The Outstanding Yachts of Sparkman & Stephens Design.* (Illus.). Norton, 1996.

Knox-Johnson, Robin. *Yachting: The History of a Passion.* (Illus.). Hearst/ Morrow, 1990.

Lane, Frederic C. *Venetian Ships and Shipbuilders of the Renaissance.* (Illus.). Reprint edition. Johns Hopkins, 1992.

Larsson, Lars. *Principles of Yacht Design.* International Marine, 1995.

Lubbock, Basil. *The Blackwall Frigates.* Brown, Son & Ferguson, Ltd., 1987.

Lubbock, Basil. *The Down Easters: American Deep-Water Sailing Ships, 1869–1929.* Dover, 1987.

Lubbock, Basil. *The Last of the Windjammers.* 2 vols. Brown, Son & Ferguson, Ltd., 1987.

Lubbock, Basil. *The Log of the Cuttysark.* Brown, Son & Ferguson, Ltd., 1987.

Lubbock, Basil. *The Nitrate Clippers.* Brown, Son & Ferguson, Ltd., 1932.

Lubbock, Basil. *Round the Horn Before the Mast.* Brown, Son & Ferguson, Ltd.

MacArthur, Robert C. *Room at the Mark: A History of the Development of Yachts, Yacht Clubs, Yacht Racing & the Racing Rules.* (Illus.). Yacht Owners, 1990.

Magoun, F. Alexander. *The Frigate Constitution & Other Historic Ships.* (Illus.). Reprint ed. Dover, 1987.

Marquardt, Karl H. *Eighteenth-Century Rigs & Rigging.* (Illus.). Phoen Pubns, 1992.

Mate, Ferenc. *Finely Fitted Yacht.* Norton, 1994.

Mate, Ferenc. *The World's Best Sailboats.* Norton, 1986.

McKay, Richard C. *Donald McKay and His Famous Sailing Ships.* Unabridged edition. (Illus.). Reprint ed. Dover, 1996.

Mendlowitz, Benjamin. *Guide to Wooden Boats: Sail.* Norton, 1996.

Morison, Samuel E. *The European Discovery of America.* 2 vols. Oxford University Press, 1993.

O'Brian, Patrick. *Men-of-War: Life in Nelson's Navy.* Norton, 1995.

O'Brian, Patrick. *The Aubrey/Maturin Novels.* Norton.

Old Sea Wings, Ways & Words in the Ways of Oak & Hemp: Sketches & Notes on Old Ships, Sails & Rigging with a Dictionary of Sea Terms. Gordon Press, 1977.

Paine, Lincoln P. *Ships of the World: An Historical Encyclopedia.* Houghton Mifflin, 1997.

Parker, Dana T. *Square Riggers in the United States & Canada: A Current Directory of Sailing Ships.* Harris, Marion, ed. Transport Trails, 1994.

Price, Anthony. *The Eyes of the Fleet: A Popular History of Frigates and Frigate Captains 1775–1815.* 2nd ed. (Illus.). Norton, 1996.

Reinders, Reinder and Paul, Kees, eds. *Carvel Construction Technique.* (Oxbow Monographs in Archaeology: No. 12). (Illus.). Oxbow Books, 1991.

Roberts-Goodson, R. Bruce. *Spray: The Ultimate Cruising Boat.* (Illus.). Sheridan, 1995.

Roger, N. A. *The Wooden World: An Anatomy of the Georgian Navy.* (Illus.). Norton, 1996.

Rousmaniere, John. *Fastnet, Force Ten.* (Illus.). Norton, 1995.

Sherwood, Richard M. *Field Guide to Sailboats.* 2nd ed. Houghton Mifflin, 1994.

Slocum, Joshua. *Sailing Alone Around the World.* McGraw-Hill, 1996.

Spectre, Peter H. and Larkin, David. *Wooden Ship: The Art, History, and Revival of Wooden Boatbuilding.* (Illus.). Houghton Mifflin, 1991.

Spurr, Daniel. *Yacht Style: Design & Decor Ideas from the World's Finest Yachts.* (Illus.). International Marine, 1990.

Stephens, William P. *Traditions and Memories of American Yachting: The Fiftieth Anniversary Edition.* McGraw-Hill, 1989.

Taylor, Roger C. *Thirty Classic Boat Designs: The Best of the Good Boats.* (Illus.). International Marine, 1992.

Underhill, Harold A., ed. *Masting and Rigging: The Clipper Ship and Ocean Carrier.* Brown, Son & Ferguson, Ltd., 1987.

Underhill, Harold. A., ed. *Sailing Ship Rigs & Rigging: With Authentic Plans of Famous Vessels.* Brown, Son & Ferguson, Ltd., 1987.

Unger, Richard W. *The Art of Medieval Technology: Images of Noah the Shipbuilder.* (Illus.). Rutgers University Press.

Unger, Richard W., ed. *Cogs, Caravels, and Galleons: The Sailing Ship 1000–1650.* (Conway's History of the Ship Series). Naval Institute Press, 1993.

Villiers, Alan. *The Quest of the Schooner Argus.* Hodder and Stoughton, 1951.

Wilbur, C. Keith. *Tall Ships of the World: An Illustrated Encyclopedia.* (Illustrated Living History Series). (Illus.). Globe Pequot, 1995.

Creole

DIRECTORIES AND ANNUALS

American Sail Training Staff and Paine, Lincoln P., eds. *Sail Tall Ships: A Directory of Sail Training & Adventure at Sea.* 9th ed. American Sail Training, 1997.

Brouwer, Norman J. *International Registry of Historic Ships.* 2nd ed. (Illus.). Sea History Press.

U.S. Sailing Staff. *Recommendations for Offshore Sailing.* (Illus.). United States Sailing Association, 1996.

United States Sailing Association 1996 Directory. (Illus.). 1996.

WoodenBoat Research Editors. *Directory of Wooden Boat Builders & Designers.* WoodenBoat Publications, 1994.

WoodenBoat Magazine Editors. *The Register of Wooden Yachts 1996–1997: A List of North American Wooden Yachts, Boats, Vessels, and Their Owners.* WoodenBoat Publications, 1996.

MANUALS AND HANDBOOKS

Ashley, Clifford W. *Ashley Book of Knots.* (Illus.). Doubleday, 1944.

Branford, Percy W. *Working in Canvas for Yachtsmen, Cadets & Sea Scouts.* Brown, Son & Ferguson, Ltd., 1987.

Casey, Don. *Canvaswork & Sail Repair.* (Illus.). McGraw-Hill, 1996.

Coles, K. Adlard. *Heavy Weather Sailing.* 4th ed. (Illus.). International Marine, 1996.

Colgate, Stephen. *Fundamentals of Sailing, Cruising & Racing.* Expanded revised edition. (Illus.). Norton, 1996.

Cornell, Jimmy. *World Cruising Handbook.* (Illus.). 3rd ed. International Marine, 1995.

Crawford, William P. *Mariner's Weather* (Illus.). Norton, 1992.

Cunliffe, Tom. *The Complete Yachtmaster: Sailing, Seamanship, & Navigation for the Modern Yacht Skipper.* 2nd ed. (Illus.). Sheridan, 1997.

Cunliffe, Tom. *Hand, Reef & Steer.* Sheridan, 1992.

Davison, Peter and Simpson, Jim, trans. *The Glenans Manual of Sailing.* (Illus.). Sterling, 1997.

Editors. *Eagle Seamanship: A Manual for Square-Rigger Sailing.* 3rd ed. Naval Institute Press, 1990.

Henderson, Richard. *Singlehanded Sailing: The Experiences & Techniques of the Lone Voyagers.* 2nd ed. (Illus.). International Marine, 1992.

Henderson, Richard. *Understanding Rigs and Rigging.* Rev. ed. (Illus.). International Marine, 1990.

Herreshoff, L. Francis. *The Complete Cruiser: The Art, Practice & Enjoyment of Boating.* (Illus.). Sheridan, 1990.

Hiscock, Eric C. *Cruising Under Sail.* 3rd ed. (Illus.). International Marine, 1987.

Howard, Jim. *Handbook of Offshore Cruising: The Dream & Reality of Modern Ocean Sailing.* (Illus.). Sheridan, 1994.

Johnson, Peter. *The Sail Magazine Book of Sailing.* (Illus.). Knopf, 1989.

Klinke, Jerry. *Rigging Handbook: The Complete Illustrated Field Reference.* (Illus.). ACRA Publishing, 1995.

Maloney, Elbert S. *Chapman's Piloting, Seamanship, & Small Boat Handling.* (Illus.). Morrow.

Marchaj, Czeslaw A. *Sail Performance: Design & Techniques to Maximize Sail Power.* (Illus.). McGraw-Hill, 1996.

Marino, Emiliano and Charbonneau, Christine. *The Sailmaker's Apprentice: A Guide for the Self-Reliant Sailor.* International Marine, 1994.

Rousmaniere, John. *The Annapolis Book of Seamanship.* Rev. ed. Simon & Schuster, 1989.

Smith, Hervey G. *Arts of the Sailor: Knotting, Splicing & Ropework.* Dover, 1990.

Toss, Brion. *The Rigger's Apprentice.* 2nd ed. (Illus.). International Marine, 1992.

Walker, Stuart H. *Advanced Racing Tactics.* (Illus.). Norton, 1986.

Walker, Stuart H. *Positioning—The Logic of Sailboat Racing.* Norton, 1992.

PERIODICALS

Boat International
Classic Boat
Cruising World
Ocean Navigator
Ships Monthly
Tall Ship International
Tall-Ship News (Association Tall-Ship Friends)
Tall Ships News (ISTA)
WoodenBoat
Yacht Capital
Yachting Monthly
Yachting World

Index of Sailing Ships

Index of People

Photographic Credits

Key: t-top; b-bottom; r-right; l-left

THE SOURCES OF THE PHOTOS ARE:

Alinari Brogi-Giraudon
15 (b, detail)

Archives Larousse-Giraudon
40 (d)

Bridgeman-Giraudon
9 (t), 15 (center), 16 (t), 19 (b), 20 (t), 22-23, 33 (b), 34 (t)

Bridgeman-Giraudon, London.
Victoria and Albert Museum 15 (t)

DPPI
7 (t), 66, 82 (l), 98, 112, 124, 185 (t)
Astorg, B.: 67 (b/l), 169
Baudin, F.: 37
Cattin, E.: 20 (b/r), 45, 55 (t), 60 (t), 61 (t), 67 (t), 75 (t), 82 (l), 83, 97, 102 (r), 103, 110, 113, 130-133, 134, 135 (l), 175, 185 (b)

Clément, F.: 36 (u, center, b/l), 181 (t)
Guéry, J.-L.: 39 (b), 56, 57 (l), 58-59
Le Pipe, P.: 11, 44 (b), 154-155, 187 (t)
Pace, F.: 8 (t), 21 (b), 35, 49, 50-51, 52 (b), 53, 70-71, 75 (center), 76 (r), 78-79, 86, 90, 95, 96, 99-101, 105 (t), 106, 111, 116, 117 (t), 118-119, 123, 126, 127 (b), 128 (l), 129, 135 (r), 136-137, 148-150, 156-157, 172-173, 176-177, 189
Pigott, B.: 50, 162-165
Stichelbault: 117 (r)
Thibault, H.: 7 (b), 48 (t), 52 (t), 55 (b), 57 (r), 65 (b), 67 (b/r), 91, 92-93, 94 (b), 104 (l), 122 (b), 142-148, 153, 184
Tienda, L. de: 77 (t), 107, 186 (t)
Tienda, M. de: 108-109
Vapillon, J.: 4-5, 20 (b/l), 36 (b/r), 42 (t), 57 (center), 61 (b), 65 (t), 74, 75 (b), 76 (u and l), 77 (b), 80, 81 (b), 82 (r), 105 (b), 117 (b), 158 (t), 161, 166, 186 (b)

Giraudon
6 (t), 8 (b), 10, 18 (detail center photo), 25 (b), 26 (b), 33 (t)

Lauros-Giraudon
9 (b), 24, 25 (t), 29, 34 (b), 39 (t)

Musée de la marine
6 (center), 6 (b), 26 (t), 41 (center and b), 42 (b)

Sea and See
41 (t)
Allisy, D.: 43, 46-47, 54, 60 (b), 72-73, 73 (b), 81 (l), 114-115, 159-160, 178-179
Borlenghi, C.: 68-69, 128 (r)
Braida, G.: 30-31, 158 (b)
Chapuis, O.: 122 (t)
Février, C.: back cover, 38 (t), 187 (b)
Forster, D.: 40 (t), 138-141
Fyot, A.: 180
Komenda, A.: cover, 19 (t), 27 (b), 28, 72, 84-85, 87, 151

Gauthier, J.: 21 (t), 62, 88-89, 182, 183 (b)
Guillemot, E.: 120, 121
Landry, M.: 125
Layani, E.: 94 (t), 102 (l), 183 (t)
Martinais, E.: 73 (t)
Martin-Raget, G.: 152-153
Pert, N.: 14, 17, 27 (u/r), 181 (b)
Wilson, A.: 27 (u/l), 48 (b), 63 (t)

Visa
Lorgnier, A.: 12-13

AND:

Levergne, P./France II Renaissance 44 (t)
Prébois, J.: 38 (b)
Puget, O.: 127 (t), 167 (r), 168 (l), 174
Roget-Viollet: 32

Art Director: Ute-Charlotte Hettler
Designer: Jacqueline Leymarie
Managing Editor: Isabelle Raimond